the

dharma flower

sutra

THE WONDERFUL DHARMA LOTUS FLOWER SUTRA.

Translated into Chinese by
Tripitaka Master Kumarajiva of Yao Ch'in

Volume 5, Chapter 4:
Belief and Understanding

with the commentary of
TRIPITAKA MASTER HUA

Translated into English by
The Buddhist Text Translation Society
San Francisco
1979

Translated by the Buddhist Text Translation Society

Primary translation: Bhikshuni Heng-yin
Reviewed by: Bhikshuni Heng-ch'ih
Edited by: Upasika Kuo-lin Lethcoe

Certified by: The Venerable Master Hua

Printed in the United States of America

First printing--1980

For information address:

        Sino American Buddhist Association
        Gold Mountain Monastery
        1731 15th Street
        San Francisco, California 94103
        U.S.A.
        (415) 621-5202
        (415) 861-9672

ISBN 0-917512-64-2

Acknowledgements:
Cover: Bhikshuni Heng-chieh
English calligraphy: Jerri-jo Idarius
Photo of the Master: Kuo-ying Brevoort
Other: Upasika Kuo-shan Anderson, Kuo Ts'an
 Epstein
Index: Bhikshuni Heng-ming

Table of Contents

The Venerable Master Hua

Translator's Introduction

In the previous volume, Chapter Three of The
Lotus Sutra, the Buddha bestows upon Shariputra a
prediction of Buddhahood. He also speaks the parable of the burning house to show how, by means
of the non-ultimate expedients of the Three
Vehicles, beings are led to the One Buddha Vehicle
and thereby escape the "burning house of the
Triple World."

In the present volume, Chapter Four: Belief
and Understanding, several disciples express
their astonishment at hearing the Buddha's
announcement of Shariputra's prediction. The
Buddha's great disciple Mahakashyapa then speaks
a parable to illustrate their feelings on the
subject:

A boy ran away from his father and wandered
in poverty and destitution for many years until,
by accident, he encountered his father again.
Although the son did not recognize his father,
the father knew he was his son and sent people
out to bring him back by force. This only frightened the poor son. The father then expediently
sent two men to offer him a job at twice the
normal wages. The son worked there for many years.
One day the wealthy man, praising the son's
honest and diligent work, rewarded him by putting
him in charge of all of his possessions. Several
more years passed and the man gathered his retinue
together and told him that the poor laborer was
actually his son and would inherit all of his
wealth. When the poor man heard this, he was
delighted and amazed, for his was beyond his
expectations entirely.

In the same way, the Sound Hearer Disciples,
headed for the goal of Arhatship, are amazed and
delighted to hear that they, too, can attain
Buddhahood. The Disciples had never hoped for
Buddhahood and had been satisfied with the small
attainments they had. The Buddha knew that they
preferred petty dharmas and didn't speak the

vii

Great Vehicle Dharma to them right away. Instead, he taught them the lesser vehicle dharmas, the Four Holy Truths, the Twelve Causal Conditions and so on. He didn't encourage them to practice the Six Perfections and the Ten Thousand Conducts.

Now, in the Dharma Flower Sutra assembly the Buddha "opens the provisional to reveal the real." He does away with former expedient devices and reveals the actual teaching of universal salvation by means of the One Buddha Vehicle.

The poor son is an analogy for the Sound Hearer Disciples and also for all of us. We, too, are capable of becoming Buddhas through the practice of the Great Vehicle Dharma. The Buddha was once a person, just like ourselves, but he cultivated, got rid of all his faults, and thereby reached Buddhahood. In the same way, if we cultivate according to Dharma, with sincerity, perseverance, and firmness, we, too, have a share in the Buddha's wisdom.

Bhikshuni Heng-yin
Co-chairperson, Primary
Translation Committee
Buddhist Text Translation
Society

December 1979
City of Ten Thousand Buddhas

viii

Editor's Introduction

Chapters IV and V of The Lotus Sutra continue the description of one of the most important
religious events in the Buddha's teaching career--
the transfer of his Two Vehicle followers to the
Great Vehicle or Buddha-path. After years of rejecting his Great Vehicle teachings as a path
applicable to themselves, the Buddha's less spirit-
ually endowed followers suddenly put forth the
aspiration for Buddhahood and discover that they
too can practice the Great Vehicle, receive the
predictions, and become Buddhas. As the Venerable
Master Hus'a commentary reveals, this event is not
limited to the disciples involved, but through
them, all those who have the merit and virtue to
hear of this wonderful event can participate in
its experience; it is a promisory event that we,
too, will receive the prediction to Buddhahood
and eventually become Buddhas.

In Chapter IV, the returning disciples tell
the story of a run-away son who after years of
fruitless wandering accidentally happens upon
his father's new home. The father recognizes
his son and, at first, attempts to use force to
keep him home; soon, however, he realizes that
force is counter-productive. Since his son is
overcome by fear and doubts by such a show of
force, he skillfully works out a plan to provide
the conditions for his son's gradual maturation.
At the appropriate time, when his son is ready
to receive the news, he reveals their true identity.

The story itself dramatically portrays how
without the Buddha's guidance, man's efforts are
fruitless, while with it, man can overcome the
fear and doubt accompanying the first stages of
awareness of the great existential gulf separating
ordinary beings from the transcendental Buddha.
Most importantly, it shows how the Buddha skillfully
teaches and transforms those willing to try,
enabling them to discard their false perceptions

ix

of themselves and realize their true identity as the Buddha's sons.

Two major themes run throughout the Venerable Master Hua's commentary. First, both the event and the story are symbolic. They are not just about some distant people, but about us, that is about everyone who has sufficient merit and virtue to in some way happen upon this Sutra. We are identified with the great disciples and son. It is we who are capable of becoming Buddhas if we but put forth the resolve to Buddhahood and repay the Buddha's kindness by diligently cultivating the Great Vehicle path. And, secondly, the Sutra text itself is one means of achieving this transformation. Each word in the event and story also has symbolic significance. For example, rice represents the emptiness of people, while flour represents the emptiness of dharmas. To help us utilize the transformatory power of the Sutra, the Venerable Master explains, in brief, the symbolic reference of each word.

Because the Sutra provides a means of reorganizing our awareness of the meaning and significance of our present lifetime, hearing and reciting the Sutra itself consitutes a major means of achieving this realization. For one who further knows what each word represents, then worshipping, reading, reciting, and studying the Sutra becomes an even more powerful aid towards achieving our ultimate realization of Buddhahood.

Upasika Kuo-lin Lethcoe
(Nancy R. Lethcoe, Ph.D.)

Chapter Four: Outline

xiv

xv

Chapter 4: Belief and Understanding

This Sutra's first chapter, the Introduction, dis-
cusses its causes and conditions. The second chapter,
Expedient Devices, tells how one within the Buddhadharma
can use various expedients to teach and transform living
beings. Because the Buddha feared that people would not
understand, he spoke the Analogy chapter to clarify the
Buddhadharma's doctrines. Although we have heard about
the expedients and the analogies, now, in the fourth chapter, Belief and Understanding, we find it is still neces-
sary to have belief.

Belief: No matter what dharma is spoken, without personal belief in it you will not be able to accept it. If you can't accept the dharma, it is just as if the dharma was not there at all. It is said,

Faith is the source of the Way and the

mother of merit and virtue;

It nurtures all our good roots.

Faith, or belief, is the beginning of the Way. It is the mother of merit and virtue. If you have faith, you can increase your good roots. If you do not have faith, you can't. So, faith is extremely important.

It is also said,

The Buddhadharma is like the great sea;

One can only enter it by means of faith.

To enter the great sea of the Buddhadharma you must have belief. If you have no belief, there is no way you can get into it.

Let's take a look at the Chinese character for the word belief, or faith: 信 hsin. On the left hand side is a standing person radical: 亻 jen. On the right hand side, we have the character for words: 言 yen. This means that there is a person there speaking. If you can't believe what he is saying, it is useless. For his words to be of use to you, you must believe them. In the same way, if you believe in the Sutras you will be able to use them to your own benefit. If you do not believe in them, you

won't. What is meant by "being able to use them to your
own benefit?" Say, for example, you have a big temper.
The Sutras say clearly that one should avoid hatred, so
you think, "Ah, I won't get angry; I shouldn't hold on to
this big temper anymore." And, you don't know quite when,
but one day you find that your temper is gone. Even if
others get angry at you, you can bear up under it. That's
faith. If you have no faith, when the Sutras say not to
get angry, you will think, "Well, that's what the Sutras
say, but who doesn't have a temper?" That's lack of
faith. Without faith you cannot obtain advantage from
the Sutra. Perhaps you think, "Well, if I listen to the
Sutras and just take everything lying down and don't get
angry, I won't obtain any advantages either. It will be
very hard to take." Hah! You may feel that there are no
advantages, but imperceptibly, by bearing up and not getting angry you gain in virtuous practice. If you get angry, you have no virtuous practice. So, your advantage
lies in gaining merit and virtue. In this regard, faith
is the most important quality.

I tell you not to have a fiery temper and not to get
angry; you agree to my face saying you will do as I say,
but as soon as you are apart from me you transform. Or,
worse yet, you continue to get angry even in my presence!
Utterly reckless, to you there is no law and no Heaven.
"He tells me not to get angry? Well, I'll just get an-

grier, and we'll see how talented I am." That's just having no faith. If you had faith you would follow my teachings.

Understanding: Once you have faith, you can gain understanding. Without faith, you can't gain understanding. The more I lecture on the Sutras, the less you believe. The less you believe, the more confused you get. The more confused you get, the less wisdom you have--you get stupid. If you give rise to faith and then understand, "Oh, I should really do as the Sutras instruct me to do," then you will have obtained advantage.

This is the fourth chapter of the Dharma Flower Sutra. Faith: Ultimately, in what does one have faith? Understanding: Ultimately, what is it that one understands? One has faith in the inconceivably wonderful Dharma of the Great Vehicle. One understands and awakens to the cultivation of the practices of the inconceivable and wonderful Great Vehicle. Thus, this Chapter is titled: Belief and Understanding.

結集法藏

處胎經云佛滅度後經七日七夜時大
迦葉告五百阿羅漢卿等五百人盡詣
十方諸佛世界阿羅漢處告以佛今涅
槃聞維已訖欲得演佛真性法身女等
速集諸賢聖微妙之言時五百羅漢以神
通力即到十方恒河沙利土集諸阿羅
漢得八億四千眾來集於此阿難一心
思惟諸應垢滅朗然大悟聖眾稱善諸
天歌歎阿難即昇高座迦葉告阿難言
佛所說法一言一字汝慎勿使有缺漏
菩薩藏集者一處聲聞藏亦集者一處
戒律藏亦集者一處闍時阿難發聲唱
言我聞如是一時佛及說佛所居處迦
葉及一切聖眾魔淚悲泣不能自勝咄
嗟老死如幻如化昨日見佛今日已稱
言為我聞最初出經胎化藏為第一中
陰藏第二摩訶衍方等藏第三戒律藏
第四十住菩薩藏第五雜藏第六金剛
藏第七佛藏第八是為釋迦牟尼佛經
法具足矣

The Venerable Ananda compiling the Sutras (See The
Dharma Flower Sutra, BTTS, 1977, Vol.II, p.69)

雞足入定

阿育王傳云尊者迦葉結集法藏已以
法付囑阿難我今欲入涅槃以法付汝
汝善守護迦葉往詣阿闍世王所相別
語守門人言大迦葉欲入涅槃故來相
語時迦葉至王三岳中坐草而坐
彌勒弟子皆見我身即時大地六種震
動迦葉將欲入定念言若阿難阿闍世
王來時山當為開令其得入若還去時
山還合釋提桓因散天香花供養迦
葉禮拜供養已乃即自合覆尊者身此
山窟神石嵌壞迦葉入滅作如是
言今日法岳崩壞法船已沒法樹已摧
法海已竭今日諸魔得大歡喜一切天
人哀戀悲泣時阿闍世王夢天梁折壞
覺已心生驚怖守門者來白王言向者
迦葉來白王欲入涅槃王聞是語與阿
難往詣雞足山山自開張供養禮拜涕
泣而還

Mahakashyapa in samadhi in Chicken Foot Mountain
(See p.869)

Sutra: T.262, 16b8

At that time the wise and long-lived Subhuti, Mahakatyayana, Mahakashyapa, Mahamaudgalyayana, having heard from the Buddha, Dharma such as they had never heard before, the bestowal of the prediction of anuttarasamyaksambodhi upon Shariputra, felt it very rare. They rose from their seats, jumped for joy, straightened their robes, bared their right shoulders, placed their right knees on the ground, singlemindedly put their palms together, inclined themselves respectfully, gazed at the Honored Countenance...

Outline:

> F2. Leading those of average
>
> dispositions to understanding.
>
> > G1. Compiler's preface tel
> >
> > ling of assembly's rejoic
> >
> > ing.

Commentary:

AT THAT TIME means right after Shakymuni Buddha had spoken the Analogies Chapter advising Shariputra that he should speak The Dharma Flower Sutra only to those to whom it is appropriate to speak it. Unless people are suited to hear it, you cannot speak it to them. This is to avoid giving unsuitable living beings a chance to

slander it. THE WISE AND LONG-LIVED SUBHUTI...Why is
Subhuti called "wise and long-lived?" The others are
listed as "Maha" or great. It's because Subhuti continues the line of the Buddha's life of wisdom. It's also
because he has received orders from one of wisdom. He is
said to take orders from the Wise One, the Buddha. In the
Prajna Dharma Assembly, the Buddha commanded Subhuti to
teach all living beings, to teach all the Bodhisattvas,
and to hand on the inheritance of Dharma. You could also
say "Mahasubhuti." He has a separate name because he is
a bit different from the others. Subhuti has three names.
He is called Good and Auspicious, Good Manifestation,
and Empty Born.

Good and Auspicious is his name because when he was
born his father called in a diviner and the diviner found
his birth to be both good and auspicious. Although he was
good and auspicious, a strange thing happened. His father
was very rich and had lots of gold, silver, and jewels in
his storehouse. But when Subhuti was born they all disappeared, and the storehouse was empty. So he was given
the name Empty Born. After seven days, all the treasures
reappeared in the storehouse, so he was also named Good
Manifestation. He was foremost of the Buddha's disciples
in understanding emptiness. He understood the doctrine of
emptiness.

"What's there to understand about emptiness?" you
ask. "Do you have to understand emptiness?"

Of course, you do. If you don't understand emptiness you don't understand the Buddhadharma. If you don't understand the Buddhadharma, you can't become a Buddha. If you want to become a Buddha, you must first understand emptiness.

"But emptiness is just nothing at all. What is there to understand?" you ask.

You must understand that "nothing at all." If you don't understand that "nothing at all," you will always be just a common person. If you understand that "nothing at all," there is unlimited benefit to be gained.

What is emptiness? Let's look at empty space. What does it mean, "empty space?" It doesn't grasp or reject or receive anything. You can't grasp it or let it go. If it took anything in, it wouldn't be empty. When Subhuti understood the doctrine of not grasping, rejecting, or receiving, he then suddenly awakened to the principle of emptiness. Although we say that there is nothing at all in emptiness, still there is something true there. Were it not for that true thing which holds up emptiness, it would long ago have broken open and been destroyed. We people don't have the talent to break open empty space and smash it to bits. If we did, that would be "realizing the Way." So the Venerable Elder Master Hsü-yün said:

> The teacup fell to the ground.
>
> Sharp and clear was its sound.

Empty space was smashed to bits,

And the mad mind was put to rest.

How did the Venerable Master Hsü-yün get enlightened?
It was in the evening, during a Ch'an session, when everyone was drinking tea. In the Ch'an Hall you hold your
small teacup in a certain way while someone pours the tea
in for you. The person who poured the tea for him knocked
his teacup out of his hand on to the floor. It made a
loud, sharp noise. The noise woke the Master from his
limitless kalpas worth of karmic consciousness. "Oh! So
that's what it's all about!" When the cup broke, what do
you think happened? Empty space disappeared. Where did
it go? Ask Master Hsü Lao. He knows where it went. And
the mad mind, the mind that climbs on conditions, the mind
which is filled with all types of ignorance, it came to
rest. It stopped. It was gone. This is what Shakyamuni
Buddha was talking about when he said,

All living beings have the Buddhanature.

All can become Buddhas. It is only because

of false thinking and attachment that they

are unable to do so.

The Shurangama Sutra says, "When the mad mind comes
to rest, it's resting is Bodhi." Your mad mind is just
your Bodhi mind, and when the mad mind stops, the Bodhi
mind arises.

MAHAKATYAYANA: "Maha" is Sanskrit and translated into

Chinese it means "great." He is "great" Katyayana. Katyayana is a Sanskrit word meaning "literary elegance,"
"fan cord," and "good shoulders" as previously explained.
He was incredibly eloquent. He could talk the dead back
into life. You have to be pretty eloquent to do that.
He was called "fan cord" because when he was young his
father died, and his mother wanted to marry again; the
child, however, was like a cord that bound her, so she
couldn't get away. He was called "good shoulders" because his shoulders were very handsome. They looked good
from the back, and even better from the front. Among the
Buddha's disciples, he is foremost in debate. No one
could out debate him. At that time there was a member
of the outside Way sect of annihilationism who challenged
him saying, "I say that when people die, they disappear.
You say they don't. I say this because of all the people
who have died, I have never heard of one who returned to
tell where they had gone, not a single one, from ancient
times to the present. They have never come back, written
a postcard, sent a telegram or made a phone call. Once
they die, it's all over. So I hold to annihilationism."

Mahakatyayana replied, "Well, let's not talk about
dead people. Let's take, for example, someone who has
broken the law and been put in jail. Does he have the
freedom to go home and tell his family where he is being
incarcerated and for how long? Is that possible?"

Because the outside Way adherent thought there was some principle in that, there was nothing he could say, except, "Supposing you are right. If someone dies and falls into the hells, they can't get out to come back for a visit. But what about those who die and supposedly go up to the heavens? Why don't they send down any news like, 'Having a wonderful time. Wish you were here?' They really should."

Mahakatyayana replied, "Let me ask you. If someone had been stuck in a pit toilet and, through great effort, managed to extricate himself, do you think he would turn around and jump back in? Compared to heaven, the world of human beings is just like a stinking pit toilet. Do you think anyone would be so stupid as to jump back in? What is more, one day in the Tushita Heaven is equal to a hundred years among people. When he got there, it would take a day to get settled and rest, another day to go sight seeing and visit the gods and receive visitors. On the third day, when he thought to return, three hundred years would have gone by back in the human world, and the people he wanted to see would have long since died.

The annihilationist was speechless. This incident proves that Mahakatyayana was truly eloquent. If you don't believe it, try debating with him yourself.

You ask, "How could I meet him?"

The Buddha transmits the Dharma to Mahakashyapa--with a flower and a smile (See <u>The</u> <u>Dharma</u> <u>Flower</u> <u>Sutra</u>, BTTS, 1977, Vol.II, p.98)

迦葉付法

付法藏經云摩訶迦葉垂涅槃時以最
勝法付囑阿難言長老當知昔世尊以
法付我年老朽將欲涅槃世間勝眼
今欲相付汝當精勤守護斯法阿難曰
諾唯然受教於是阿難演暢妙法化諸
眾生就其宿命有大功德今當隨順說
其因緣乃住古世定光如來時為沙門
嘗一沙彌教令讀誦當此沙彌為師
廢若經少稽留即便呵責時此沙彌為師
乞食若少稽留經不充限遺師罵詈於
是沙彌甚為愁惱當乞食際且行且誦
時有長者怪而問之沙彌具答如上長
者言勿憂但勤誦習我當供給從此沙
彌得專讀誦經常充足爾時沙彌即世
尊是施食長者阿難是也以斯福緣智
慧深妙總持強識多聞宏廣不可稱計
迦葉告曰長老若入涅槃王舍城
有長者名商那和修已於過去深種善
根可度出家付以法藏

The First Patriarch Mahakashyapa transmits the Dharma
to the Second Patriarch, Arya Ananda (See The Dharma
Flower Sutra, BTTS, 1977, Vol.II., p.99)

He's right here in The Dharma Flower Sutra. He's
right in front of you, and you can't see him. Who are you
going to complain to about that? He's right in front of
you. This Venerable One has come to our Buddha Hall.
Subhuti is here, and Mahakatyana is here, and Mahakashyapa
is here. If you can't see them, whose fault is it?

MAHAKASHYAPA: Mahakashyapa was the first Buddhist
Patriarch. He is still in the world and has not entered
Nirvana. Why not? He's waiting for Maitreya Bodhisattva
to become a Buddha, at which time he will give the bowl,
given him by the Four Heavenly Kings, to Maitreya. The
Patriarch is now in China, Yünnan Province, Chicken Foot
Mountain in samadhi waiting for Maitreya. "Maha," again
means great. Kashyapa is Sanskrit and means "light drinking clan." His body emitted light of purple-gold color
which covered over all other light--sunlight, moonlight,
starlight, lamplight. He outshone them all. It was as
if all other light had been, so to speak, swallowed up by
his light. This is an analogy. He didn't really drink
light. Why did his body emit this light? It was because
limitless aeons ago, following the Nirvana of Vipashyin
Buddha, and during that Buddha's Dharma-image age, he saw
an image of that Buddha. The gold had all peeled off of
the Buddha. At that time a woman went out and took up a
collection to regild the image. She went to a goldsmith
with the money saying, "I want to regild this Buddha image. How much would you charge?" The Goldsmith, admir-

ing her very much for her good heart, said, "You shouldn't
take the merit and virtue all for yourself. We should
share it. I will do it for half the price I normally
charge, and we can split the merit and virtue." The image was regilded and because of the merit and virtue obtained from that deed, in every life he was born with a
body that was golden, outshining all other kinds of light.
After they gilded the image, since they had such close
affinities, they got married. The woman also had a golden
body. They vowed that in every life they would be married
and propogate the Buddhadharma. So, during the time of
Shakyamuni Buddha they were also husband and wife and then
left home to cultivate the Way. Now, you should not mis-
understand. Although they were married, it was only in
name. They weren't married in deed, because they both
cultivated the Way and they weren't like ordinary married
people who give rise to so much ignorance and engage in
impure activities. How do we know this? Because their
bodies both emitted golden light. If they had indulged
in marital relations they would not have emitted golden
light whether or not they regilded the Buddha image.
Unless they protected their merit and virtue in their
actions, they would not have been able to keep their
light.

Mahakashyapa's name also means "great turtle clan."
This is because his forefathers saw a huge turtle with a
diagram on its back telling them how to cultivate the

Way. Mahakashyapa's parents prayed in front of a tree
to the tree spirit seeking a son, and he was born. He
is also called "Pippala," then, which was the name of
the tree. When he was in his twenties, his parents wanted to find him a wife. He said, "I won't marry any ordinary woman. It must be a woman whose body is the same
color as mine." After a time, his parents found such a
woman in another country, and they were married and cultivated the Way together. He was a member of an outside
Way sect that worshipped fire. He cultivated the skill
of fire. For example, he did things like walking on fire.
He took fire as a god, making offerings and bowing to it.
Whenever he saw fire he said, "Fire is god. Look, anything that gets in the fire dies. Fire is just god."
He bowed to fire. When he was 102 years old, he met the
Buddha. After the Buddha got enlightened, he first
crossed over the five Bhikshus. Then he took a look and
saw that in Magadha there was a great immortal, Mahakashyapa. If he crossed over Mahakashyapa, all of his disciples would become Buddhist disciples. He went and
spoke the Dharma to Kashyapa. Kashyapa thought his own
skill was very highly developed, but no matter what he
did, he couldn't outdo the Buddha. So he bowed to the
Buddha as his teacher and cultivated ascetic practices,
becoming foremost of the disciples in cultivation of ascetic practices. There are twelve types of ascetic prac-

tices. The Buddha noticed that as old as Kashyapa was, he was still eating once a day and sleeping under a tree and so on, and told him to discontinue his bitter practices. Kashyapa didn't waver, however, he just kept on cultivating them. So Shakyamuni Buddha praised him saying that his bitter practices were insuring that the Buddhadharma would dwell long in the world.

MAHAMAUDGALYAYANA: His name means "descendant of a family of bean gatherers." It also means "turnip root." He is foremost in spiritual penetrations. Because he had great spiritual penetrations, one time he decided to use his spiritual powers and go off to the east through limitless, limitless worlds, but he still couldn't find a place where the Buddha's voice did not reach. He was also very filial. Now in the world, every year on the 15th day of the 7th lunar month, we celebrate the Ullambana Assembly. This came about because of Maudgalyayana. When he obtained the six spiritual penetrations and the five eyes, he first took a look to see where his parents had gone. He saw that his mother had fallen into the unintermittent hells. She was skin and bones and undergoing tremendous suffering. He took a bowl of food to her. She took the bowl with one hand and covered it with the sleeve of her other hand, fearing that the other ghosts would see it and try to take it away from her. But as soon as she put a bite of food in her mouth, it turned

into burning coals! She couldn't eat it. Why did it turn
into fire? Because her karmic obstacles were too heavy.
Everything people encounter is a manifestation of their
karmic obstacles. Because her karmic obstacles were so
heavy, this very good food turned into fire. Maudgalyayana, despite all his spiritual powers, had no way to save
his mother, so he hurried back to the Buddha and asked
for help. The Buddha said, "When your mother was alive,
she ate a lot of fish roe. She also slandered the Triple
Jewel and was disrespectful towards the Sangha. That's
why she fell into hell. Even though you have certified
to the fruit of Arhatship, you cannot save her. What's
to be done? You should invite the Sangha of the ten directions on the 15th day of the 7th lunar month, which
is the day of the Buddha's rejoicing and the day of the
Sangha's rest, their vacation. You see, because the Buddha is happy on that day, he doesn't watch over the Sangha, and so they can do just about whatever they want.
If they want to go out into the streets, they can; if
they want to sleep, they can; if they want to cook, they
can. Usually, they are very disciplined, but on this day
they relax, because it is the end of the Summer Retreat
which lasts from the 15th day of the 4th month to the
15th day of the 7th month. During these three months,
they are not allowed to go outside. They can't walk on
the ground; they have to stay in their dwellings. On the

15th of the 7th month they are "liberated" and can go out again. Why aren't they allowed to go walking around outside? Is that a crime? No. It's because during that time of year there are many, many bugs on the roads. If they walked on the ground, they would sqaush them. Since they don't want to kill, they avoid going anywhere during this time.

Shakyamuni Buddha told Mahamaudgalyayana to invite all the Sangha of the ten directions to gather together on the 15th day of the 7th month and make offerings to them. In this way his mother could leave suffering, attain bliss, and be born in the heavens. He did just that, and his mother was reborn in the heavens. After that, every year on that day they conducted the Ullambana Dharma Assembly so that other living beings could save their parents who had committed offenses and fallen into the hells and cross them over so they could be reborn in the heavens. The Ullambana ceremony is still conducted every year. Ullambana means "releasing those who are hanging upside down." People in the hells are as if hanging upside down by a rope. On this day they are cut loose, liberated.

Mahamaudgalyayana's personal name was Kolita, which is also the name of a tree. His father and mother also prayed to a tree spirit seeking a son.

HAVING HEARD FROM THE BUDDHADHARMA SUCH AS THEY HAD

NEVER HEARD BEFORE/ These four Venerable Ones heard Dharma from the Buddha that they had never heard before. THE BESTOWAL OF THE PREDICTION OF ANNUTARASAMYAKSAMBODHI UPON SHARIPUTRA/ They figured that since they were Shariputra's colleagues, and he received the enlightenment prediction, for sure they all had a share. They FELT IT VERY RARE/ Their hearts awakened to and understood what was going on. THEY ROSE FROM THEIR SEATS, JUMPED FOR JOY/ What made them jump right up in the air for joy? It was their limitless aeon's worth of habits. For limitless aeons, when people are happy they have danced around, skipped like children. That they rose from their seats represents purity of body karma. That they felt it was very rare represents purity of mind karma. STRAIGHTENED THEIR ROBES/ This represents that they put down the Small Vehicle doctrines and picked up the Great Vehicle Buddhadharma. BARED THEIR RIGHT SHOULDERS/ This represents the opening of the provisional to reveal the real. Earlier, before the provisional had been opened, it was as if the right shoulder was covered. Now, baring the shoulder represents opening the provisional. PLACED THEIR RIGHT KNEES ON THE GROUND/ The ground represents the real dharma, the real wisdom. PUT THEIR PALMS TOGETHER SINGLEMINDEDLY/ represents the non-duality of the provisional and the real. The provisional is just the real, and the real is just the provisional. One opens the provisional to reveal the real, and for the sake of the real one bestows the provisional.

Opening the provisional to reveal the real.

the real is contained in the provisional.

Bestowing the provisional for the sake of

the real, the provisional is contained

in the real.

Their putting their palms together singlemindedly represents the negation of both provisional and real because
they are non-dual, and therefore, there is no provisional
or real.

INCLINED THEMSELVES RESPECTFULLY/ They inclined their
their bodies. Basically, their bodies weren't entirely
straight or bent. But they can bend, and they can
straighten out again. This represents the assertion of
both the provisional and real. Whatever is provisional
is real, and whatever is real is just provisional.

GAZED AT THE HONORED COUNTENANCE represents "we turn
from provisional teachings and go towards the Buddha's
Real teachings." Previously, we studied the Small Vehicle. Now, in the presence of the Buddha, we come to
study the real Dharma, real wisdom.

Sutra: T. 16 b 12
. . . And spoke to the Buddha, saying,
"We, who dwell at the head of the Sangha
and are advanced in years, told ourselves
that we had already attained Nirvana
and had no further responsibility, and
we did not go forward to seek anuttarasamyaksambodhi.

Outline:

> G2. An explanation for the Buddha.
>> H1. Explanation of attaining understanding
>> in prose and verse.
>>> I1. Prose
>>>> J1. Understanding through Dharma.
>>>>> K2. Speaking of Dharma proper.
>>>>>> L1. Based on former understan-
>>>>>> ding they did not seek further.
>>>>>>> M1. Statement.

Commentary:

AND SPOKE TO THE BUDDHA SAYING/ is the purity of the
mouth karma. "WE, WHO DWELL AT THE HEAD OF THE SANGHA"/
We refers to Subhuti, Mahakatyayana, Mahakashyapa, and Mahamaudgalyayana. These four dwelt at the head of the Sangha. Why didn't these people seek the Great Vehicle Buddhadharma, the Buddha Vehicle? They were the leaders of
the Sangha and models for others. They understood the
Buddhadharma at a very high level. They had left home
for a great many years. Those who have left home and just
received precepts are called new-preceptees. Those who
have held the precepts for many years are called old-
preceptees. Their precept age is advanced. These four
were very lofty, and those who came after them imitated
them. Because they were the models for others, they felt
that if they suddenly changed their course of thought and

decided to cast the Small Vehicle aside to study the Great
Vehicle, thus changing their principles, then those who
followed them would not believe in them. They would say,
"Look at that. They're really not reliable. They aren't
cultivating the Small Vehicle any more; they've switched
to the Great Vehicle." They were afraid others would ri-
dicule them. Thus, they stubbornly held on to the Small
Vehicle and refused to change. They were looking out for
others, too, fearing that, if they changed, others would
lose their faith in them and retreat from their resolve
for the Way. Thus, they didn't seek the Great Vehicle.
However, because they clung to the Small Vehicle, they
could not understand the Great Vehicle. Why didn't they
wish to put aside their hearts for the Small Vehicle?
They didn't know that the three provisional vehicles were
opened to reveal the one real vehicle. The Sound Hearer,
Conditioned Enlightened, and the Bodhisattva Vehicles are
the three provisional vehicles. They were opened to reveal the one Buddha Vehicle, but they were unaware of
this and stubbornly held to these lesser vehicles. With
this stubborn attachment to the Small Vehicle, they were
unable to change. Both their stubborn attachment and
their desire to remain consistent so that others would
not lose faith constituted their first mistake.

The second reason they did not seek the Great Vehicle was because they were ADVANCED IN YEARS. If they
were to practice the Bodhisattva Path, they would be re-

quired to save themselves, to save others, and vastly
save all living beings. Now, they were so old they HAD
NO FURTHER RESPONSIBILITY. They were so old they felt
there was nothing much they could do at their age, and so
they didn't seek the Great Vehicle. They looked down upon
themselves, thinking themselves to old to try to certify
to the Buddha fruit. "We're too old; we're useless," they
thought. Since they couldn't break through this attachment, they had the false view that they could not be ex-
pected to seek the Buddha Vehicle, the Great Vehicle Buddhadharma.

Thirdly, they thought that they HAD ALREADY ATTAINED
NIRVANA, so they figured they didn't need to seek the
Great Vehicle Dharma. Although they had attained Nirvana,
that Nirvana was merely a one-sided nirvana with residue.
It was not ultimate Nirvana. They thought, "Lotuses do
not grow on the high ground; they only grow in the low
places in the water." Since they had entered the proper
position and obtained the unconditioned, attained Nirvana,
they did not bring forth the resolve for the Great Vehicle.
Previously, they had not understood the provisional dharma.
That is why they thought that they had attained the proper
position when they had not attained the ultimate Nirvana
at all. Because of this minor attachment on their part,
they didn't know that they were already cultivating the
Bodhisattva Path.

These were three reasons why they DID NOT GO FORWARD

TO SEEK ANUTTARASAMYAKSAMBODHI, the Buddha fruit, utmost
right and perfect enlightenment.

Sutra: T. 16 b 15

The World Honored One has, from of old, been speaking the Dharma for a long time. Sitting here all this time, our bodies tired, we have merely been mindful of emptiness, signlessness, and wishlessness, taking no delight in the Bodhisattva-Dharmas, in their samadhis of playfulness, in their purification of Buddha-lands, or in their maturation of living beings. What is the reason? The World Honored One has led us to escape the three realms and attain certification to Nirvana. Besides, we are now advanced in years and when the Buddha taught the Bodhisattvas of anuttara-samyaksambodhi we did not give rise to even a single thought of longing for it.

Outline:

M2. Explanation.

Commentary:

The four Elders speak to the World Honored One: "THE
WORLD HONORED ONE HAS, FROM OF OLD, BEEN SPEAKING THE DHARMA
FOR A LONG TIME." It's been a long time and the Buddha has
spoken Dharma continuously. SITTING HERE ALL THIS TIME,
we old folks find OUR BODIES TIRED. We've been sitting so
long we got lazy and nodded off during the lectures. Don't
think that nodding off and entering samadhi are the same

thing! In samadhi your head doesn't lean this way or that, front or back. It's a very clear and lucid state; it's not being half asleep thinking the lectures are too tiring; that's just cheating yourself. Hah!

"WE HAVE MERELY BEEN MINDFUL OF EMPTINESS, SIGNLESSNESS, AND WISHLESSNESS. Everything is emptiness, signless, and there is nothing to be done. It's empty, and we don't want any marks. Therefore, we don't need to practice the activity of the Bodhisattva Path or do merit and virtue. We don't wish for anything at all." That's what they said, and therefore they found themselves TAKING NO DELIGHT IN THE BODHISATTVA DHARMAS, THEIR SAMADHIS OF PLAYFULNESS, that is, their use of various spiritual powers to teach and transform living beings. THEIR PURIFICATION OF BUDDHA LANDS, purifying the lands and THEIR MATURATION OF LIV-ING BEINGS, helping living beings to realize their vows and wishes. They took no delight in these things; they weren't the least bit interested in them; they wanted no-thing to do with them. Totally uninterested! That's called "being stubborn" again. They thought they were just fine the way they were. They were satisfied with just a small portion of what they could have had.

"WHAT IS THE REASON? Why didn't we seek the Great Vehicle Buddhadharma, that wondrous doctrine? THE WORLD HONORED ONE HAS LED US TO ESCAPE THE THREE REALMS, AND ATTAIN CERTIFICATION TO NIRVANA. The World Honored One has said that we have left the Three Realms and certified

to the attainment of Nirvana. BESIDES, WE ARE NOW AD-

VANCED IN YEARS. We're old already. We're so old we can

hardly walk! AND WHEN THE BUDDHA TAUGHT THE BODHISATTVAS

OF ANUTTARASAMYAKSAMBODHI, WE DID NOT GIVE RISE TO EVEN A

SINGLE THOUGHT OF LONGING FOR IT. Really, we like it the

way we are; we're satisfied. We could care less."

Sutra: T. 16 b 21

Now, in the presence of the Buddha, having
heard him bestow upon the Sound Hearers the
anuttarasamyaksambodhi prediction, our
hearts rejoice enthusiastically and we obtain what we never have had. We never
thought that now we would suddenly be
able to hear this rare Dharma. We rejoice
profoundly, having gained great and good
benefit.

Outline:

L2. Attainment in

the present assembly.

Commentary:

NOW, IN THE PRESENCE OF THE BUDDHA, HAVING HEARD HIM,

Shakyamuni Buddha BESTOW UPON THE SOUND HEARERS, upon

Shariputra, this includes the Conditioned Enlightened Ones

and the Bodhisattvas as well. THE ANUTTARASAMYAKSAMBODHI

PREDICTION, a prediction for their attainment of the ut-

most right and perfect enlightenment OUR HEARTS REJOICE
ENTHUSIASTICALLY seeing Shariputra receive a prediction,
and knowing that he is our peer; we know that we can also
attain one. AND WE OBTAIN WHAT WE NEVER HAVE HAD. We never
heard this Buddhadharma before. WE NEVER THOUGHT, it never would have occurred to us, THAT NOW, SUDDENLY WE WOULD
BE ABLE TO HEAR THIS RARE DHARMA, The Wonderful Dharma
Lotus Flower Sutra, that wonderful Dharma. WE REJOICE
PROFOUNDLY, we are really lucky indeed! They are delighted HAVING ATTAINED THIS GREAT AND GOOD BENEFIT.

Sutra: T. 16 b 23
It is as if, without our seeking them, limitless precious gems had come into our possession.

Outline:

> K2. Making reference to
> the analogy.

Commentary:

'IT IS AS IF, WITHOUT OUR SEEKING THEM, LIMITLESS PRE-
CIOUS GEMS HAD COME INTO OUR POSSESSION, so many Dharma
gems, and we didn't need to seek for them. We just got
them without asking." When Shariputra received a prediction, they knew they had a share in it. They weren't ex-
cluded. They, too, were sure to obtain a prediction for
the utmost, right and perfect enlightenment from the Buddha.

Sutra: T. 16 b 25
World Honored One, we would now like to
speak a parable to clarify this principle.

Outline:

> > J2. Understanding through
> > analogy.
> > > K1. Setting up the anal-
> > > ogy.
> > > > L1. Expressing the
> > > > wish to speak.

Commentary:

"WORLD HONORED ONE, WE WOULD NOW LIKE TO SPEAK A
PARABLE, we are delighted to do so in order TO MAKE CLEAR
THIS MEANING."

Sutra: T 16 b 25
It is as if there were a person who, in
his youth, left his father and ran away,
dwelling long in another country, perhaps
ten, twenty or even fifty years.

Outline:

> > L2. Setting up the analogy pro-
> > per.
> > > M1. Father and son are se-
> > > parated.

N1. Son turns his back
on father and runs away.
O1. Turning his back
on father and running
off.

Commentary:

"IT IS AS IF THERE WERE A PERSON WHO, IN HIS YOUTH...
Youth means that his good roots were few and weak, very
scanty. LEFT HIS FATHER AND RAN AWAY. Having scanty good
roots, he was not disposed to the Great Vehicle, and so
he left his father. The father represents the Thus Come
One's response body. During the time of twenty thousand
million Buddhas, Shakyamuni Buddha taught living beings;
however, after Shakyamuni Buddha's response body went to
Nirvana and the living beings were separated from their
teacher, they all retreated from the Great Vehicle mind.
Basically, Shakyamuni Buddha taught them at that time to
cultivate the Great Vehicle Dharma. However, once they
were separated from the World Honored One, they retreated
from the Great Vehicle disposition. They left their father.

They RAN: This means that they covered themselves
with ignorance. They ran AWAY means that they headed for
birth and death.

DWELLING LONG IN ANOTHER COUNTRY...The other country
refers to the triple realm of desire, the form realm, and
the formless realm. They got caught up in the five de-

sires: wealth, sex, fame, food, and sleep. They got
caught up and forgot to return: FOR PERHAPS TEN...Ten refers to the gods. TWENTY refers to the human realm. OR
EVEN FIFTY YEARS...Fifty years refers to the five paths:
the gods, humans, hell-beings, hungry ghosts, and animals.
Asuras are not included, because they are found in each
of the five realms. Living beings in the triple realm do
not know that they should cultivate the Dharma door which
leads to escape.

Sutra: T. 16b 27

As he grew older, he became poor and
needy and ran about in the four directions
in search of clothing and food. Gradually
he wandered until he accidentally approached his native land.

Outline:

> 02. Returning towards
>
> the origin.

Commentary:

This describes the Great Vehicle disposition. In the
past, they had received the Buddha's teaching. Although
they had retreated from the thought of the Great Vehicle,
still the seeds of the Great Vehicle imperceptibly remained and grew. Therefore, the text says, AS HE GREW OL-
DER. The Great Vehicle potential was just about ready.

Even though the Great Vehicle seeds had more or less matured, still their blessings in the Great Vehicle were a-
bout to run out. How could their Great Vehicle seeds be
growing and their blessings run out at the same time?
It was because they retreated from the Great Vehicle and
cultivated the small vehicle. So, the more they cultivated, the poorer and more needy they got. They were
destitute because they lacked blessings and virtue.

HE BECAME POORER. They were poor from having undergone the eight sufferings: birth, old age, sickness,
death, the suffering of being separated from what one
loves, the suffering of being together with what one hates,
the suffering of not attaining what one seeks, and the
suffering of the raging blaze of the five skandhas. In
the three realms, they had undergone all these eight sufferings because they did not know how to seek a way to
escape the three realms. They were oppressed by the eight
sufferings and so they were poor. They were poor AND
NEEDY, that is, they were attacked on all sides by the
eight sufferings. There was suffering to the left of them,
suffering to the right of them, suffering in front, be-
hind, and all around them. It was as if they were being
burned by a fire on all sides. They were poor and needy
because they had retreated from the Great Vehicle and were
burned by the fire of the eight sufferings.

AND RAN ABOUT IN THE FOUR DIRECTIONS. The four directions refers to the Four Applications of Mindfulness with regard to body, feelings, thoughts, and dharmas. They had been through all of the Four Applications of mindfulness, running about therein.

IN SEARCH OF CLOTHING AND FOOD. This represents that they were seeking the food of the proper Path and the clothing of the Aids to the Path.

GRADUALLY, HE WANDERED, taking his time step by step, day by day. Originally, he had run off a long way to another country. Having run so far and grown older, passing a year in each country, he made his way back to his own country. UNTIL HE ACCIDENTALLY APPROACHED HIS NATIVE LAND. He didn't do it intentionally; it was by accident. This represents the bitter practices cultivated by those of outside way religions. Basically, they are incorrect, but sometimes they can create a causal affinity enabling them to receive the proper teaching. For example, after Shakyamuni Buddha realized Buddhahood,

he went everywhere and crossed over those of outside ways, leading them to be the first to attain the Way and gain liberation.

Sutra: T. 16b28

His father, from the first, had set out seeking his son but in vain. He settled midway in a city. His household was one of great wealth, with limitless wealth and jewels, gold, silver, lapis lazuli, coral, amber, crystal, pearls, and other jewels. His granaries and treasuries were overflowing, and he had many servants, ministers and assistants, as well as countless elephants, horses, carriages, cattle, and sheep. The profits from his trade extended to the other countries, and there were also many traders and merchants.

Outline:

N2. Father seeks

son and stops

halfway.

Commentary:

HIS FATHER, FROM THE FIRST, HAD SET OUT SEEKING HIS SON BUT IN VAIN. The father is the Buddha. The Buddha taught living beings, but they did not cultivate the Great Vehicle. They preferred to cultivate the Small Vehicle. They ran far, far away to another country. The Buddha set out searching for them but did not find them. The Buddha was looking for his disciples, but they didn't have the potential for the Great Vehicle, so they did not meet up with him; he sought them in vain. HE SETTLED MIDWAY IN A

CITY. Midway means halfway between the Adorned Land of Real Reward and the Land of Expedients with Residue. He stopped there and did not continue to speak the Dharma and teach living beings. The city he stopped in was that of nirvana with residue. However, HIS HOUSEHOLD WAS ONE OF GREAT WEALTH. Although the Buddha wanted to enter Nirvana, he thought it over: "I have so many Dharma treasures and have no one to pass them on to. Who am I going to give them to?" The great wealth refers to the Three Storehouses and Twelve Divisions of the Canon and all the limitless treasures of the Dharma.

WITH LIMITLESS WEALTH AND JEWELS, GOLD, SILVER, LAPIS LAZULI, CORAL, AGATE CRYSTAL, AND PEARLS, which are more or less like as-you-will pearls. If you obtain one, everything is as you wish it to be AND OTHER JEWELS of all kinds. This represents the Buddha's Thirty-seven Wings of Enlightenment as well as the Four Truths, Twelve Links, and the Six Perfections—all the Dharma treasures.

HIS GRANARIES, where the grain was stored, AND THE TREASURIES where gems were stored represent the Buddha's treasury being filled with limitless Dharma jewels.

AND HE HAD MANY SERVANTS which represent the expedient dharmas. They will do any work you ask them to do. They will sweep the floor or cook or do other work. Expedients are used in many ways.

MINISTERS means great ministers.

ELEPHANTS represent the Three Contemplations in a single thought of the Great Vehicle: There is no order in contemplations--they are done simultaneously. Emptiness is falseness and falseness is emptiness and so on. The very emptiness is itself falseness, is itself the middle. This is cultivated by the Bodhisattvas of the Perfect Teaching whose dispositions are very quick and who do not need to cultivate step by step. It is the Dharma door of the Sudden Teaching. They certify to attainment immediately.

HORSES represent the Three Contemplations in succession: First, one contemplates emptiness, after that falseness, and after that, the middle. This guides Bodhisattvas of the Special Teaching to the position of the Great Vehicle. They cultivate step by step.

CATTLE represents the two contemplations of substantive emptiness and analyzed emptiness and leads Bodhisattvas of the Pervasive Teaching to the Great Vehicle.

SHEEP represent the analyzation of Dharmas for self-cultivation and leads the Sound Hearers to the Great Vehicle. The Conditioned Enlightened Vehicle is not mentioned because when a Buddha is appearing in the world, the Sound Hearers and the Conditioned Enlightened Ones can be lumped together with "Sound Hearers." COUNTLESS means that there were countless beings of the Small Vehicle.

THE PROFITS FROM HIS TRADE. Trade means literally going and coming. "Going" refers to the doctrine that the mind gives rise to the ten thousand dharmas. "Coming" refers to the doctrine that the ten thousand dharmas return to the mind. "Profits" refers to teaching and transforming living beings who attain benefit thereby. It's like interest in the bank. When living beings are saved and led to the Great Vehicle position, it's like they collect interest. EXTENDED TO THE OTHER COUNTRIES, that is, filled the three realms.

TRADERS are businessmen who travel around. MERCHANTS refers to those who stay in one place and do business. THERE WERE ALSO MANY...The traders and merchants represent those of Great and Small Vehicle dispositions, the Bodhisattvas and Sound Hearers being present in large numbers.

Sutra: T. 16c2
Then the poor son, having wandered through various villages and passed through countries and cities, at last reached the city where his father had settled.

Outline:

N3. Son reaches the city where his father is living.

Commentary:

THEN THE POOR SON, that is, those of the two vehicles, HAVING WANDERED THROUGH VARIOUS VILLAGES, that is, running around in the burning house of the three realms, AND PASSED THROUGH COUNTRIES AND CITIES, having travelled in many paths, through many different lands and small settlements, AT LAST REACHED THE CITY WHERE HIS FATHER HAD SETTLED. Unknowingly, he arrived at the city where his father was living.

Tomorrow is the anniversary of Kuan Yin's leaving home, the 19th day of the 6th lunar month. The Bodhisattva has three anniversaries each year and you should remember them. If you don't remember them, it indicates that you don't really have faith in Kuan Yin Bodhisattva. For example, in China we say, "You should know your parents' age. So you can sigh and know fear." This means, that you should know how old your parents are in order to be filial to them. When you know, for example, that your father is eighty years old you will be very happy and sigh, "Ah! He's a ripe old age." On a level deeper you will be afraid. Of what? "He's eighty already. He'll soon die. My father will leave me soon." We should be just as filial to the Buddhas and Bodhisattvas and know, for example, the Buddha's birthday is the 8th day of the 4th month. The anniversary of the Buddha's realizing the Way is the 8th day of the 12th month. The day of the

894

Buddha's entry into Nirvana is the 15th of the 2nd month. The anniversary of the Buddha's leaving home is the 8th day of the 2nd month. These you should remember.

Kuan Yin Bodhisattva has special affinities with all of us living beings in the Saha world. So we should always remember these dates. What is more, on each anniversary, students of the Buddhadharma should come and do acts of merit and virtue. On these anniversaries or on the 1st and 15th of the lunar months, if you do merit and virtue or make offerings to the Triple Jewel the merit and virtue is greater by hundreds of thousands of tens of thousands of times.

Sutra: T. 16c5

The father had always been mindful of his son. Although they had been separated for over fifty years, he had never spoken of the matter to anyone, but merely pondered over it, his heart filled with regret, as he thought, 'I am old and decrepit. I have much wealth: gold, silver, and precious gems, granaries and storehouses filled to overflowing. Such a pity that I have no son! One day I'm bound to die, and when I do, my wealth will be scattered and lost, for I have no one to bequeath them to.' This is why he ever earnestly thought of his son. 'If I could only get my son back, I'd make him heir to my wealth. I'd be contented and happy and have no further worries.'

迦葉求度

因果經云偷羅厥义國有一婆羅門名
曰迦葉極大智慧誦四章陀論其家巨
富善能布施其婦端正舉國無雙夫婦
二人無有欲想不樂在家厭離世間思
惟求訪出家之法即捨家業入於山林
心念口言諸佛如來出家修道我今亦
當隨佛出家即便脫去金縷織衣而著
壞色衲衣自剃鬚髮爾時諸天於虛空
中現見迦葉自其名薩婆燕達出家學
道號為釋迦牟尼佛今在竹園中住迦
葉聞天語已即往禮之即行遂達迦葉即
當來宜往度之即行遂達迦葉知其
便頂禮佛足白佛言是我大師我是弟
子佛言迦葉當知五陰色身是大苦聚
迦葉聞已即便見諦乃至得於阿羅漢
果爾時世尊即與迦葉俱還竹園以此
迦葉有大威德天人所重故名大迦葉
乃至佛滅住持法化被於來世此人之
力也

Mahakashyapa asks the Buddha to take him across.
(See The Dharma Flower Sutra, BTTS, 1977, Vol.II, p.95)

證明說咒

大悲經云釋迦牟尼佛在補陀洛迦山
觀世音宮殿寶莊嚴道場中坐寶師子
座時觀世音菩薩密放神通光明照耀
世界天宮龍宮皆悉震動時觀世音菩
薩白佛言我有是悲心陀羅尼今當故
說為諸眾生得安樂故除一切病得壽
命故得富饒故滅一切惡業重罪遠離
怖畏速能滿足諸希求故唯願世尊慈
哀聽許佛言今正是時宜應速說復白
佛言若有四眾弟子誦持者起大悲心先
當至心稱念我之名字然後當誦此
神咒此咒能除滅身中一切重罪若諸
眾生誦持大悲神咒於現在生中一
切所求若不果遂者不得為大悲心陀
羅尼也觀世音菩薩於眾會前合掌正
住於諸眾生起大悲心即說神妙章句
陀羅尼說此咒已天雨寶花繽紛而下
十方諸佛悉皆歡喜天魔外道恐怖毛
豎一切眾會皆獲果證一無量眾生發菩
提心

Kuan-yin Bodhisattva speaks the Great Compassion Mantra
for Shakyamuni Buddha in the palace at Potala Mtn. (See
The Dharani Sutra, BTTS, 1976, p.22)

Outline:

> N4. His father
> worries.

Commentary:

THE FATHER HAD ALWAYS BEEN MINDFUL OF HIS SON, that
is, the Buddha constantly recollects his disciples, he
always recollects the living beings with the disposition
of the Great Vehicle. AND ALTHOUGH THEY HAD BEEN SEPARA-
TED, the living beings the Buddha taught had been separated from him for over fifty years. "Fifty years" represents the Five Paths: gods, humans, hungry ghosts, animals,
and hell-beings. BUT HAD NEVER SPOKEN OF THE MATTER TO
ANYONE. For such a long time the Buddha never told anyone
about this. He never told anyone that his Small Vehicle
living beings had left their father and run away from home.
Did the Bodhisattvas know about it? Yes. But, since the
Buddha never talked about it, they never brought it up.
The Great Vehicle Bodhisattvas know that the further the
small vehicle people ran, the further off they'd get. And
yet the Buddha never talked about this. BUT MERELY PON-
DERED OVER IT, HIS HEART FILLED WITH REGRET. "Oh, why
didn't I teach them more doctrine before, so that they
wouldn't retreat from their Great Vehicle resolve?" He
was upset because the children were simply too stupid.
Those of the two vehicles didn't know enough to come back
home, that is, to return to the Buddha.

AS HE THOUGHT, "I AM OLD AND DECREPIT. I have about
finished teaching and transforming living beings. I HAVE
MUCH WEALTH, Dharma wealth, Dharma treasures, GOLD, SIL-
VER, PRECIOUS GEMS, all the various Dharma gems, GRANA-
RIES represent all the Dhyana samadhis. STOREHOUSES re-
present the real mark wisdom. FILLED TO OVERFLOWING.
SUCH A PITY I HAVE NO SON! I have no disciple. ONE DAY
I'M BOUND TO DIE, AND WHEN I DO, MY WEALTH WILL BE SCAT-
TERED AND LOST. I have so many Dharma treasures and
no one to inherit them. When I enter into Nirvana, they
will be scattered and lost. AND NO ONE TO BEQUEATH THEM
TO." The Buddha sighs to himself for he couldn't find any-
one to inherit his wealth, and so he was very nervous.
THIS IS WHY HE EVER EARNESTLY THOUGHT OF HIS SON. He
thought of his disciples. "IF I COULD GET MY SON BACK.
My living beings with Great Vehicle dispositions, I'D MAKE
HIM HEIR TO MY WEALTH, transmit the Dharma to them, pass
the Dharma treasures on to them. I WOULD BE CONTENTED
AND HAPPY AND HAVE NO FURTHER WORRIES." Having gotten
what he wished for, he would be extremely happy and tran-
quil. With an heir to inherit the Dharma, the Buddha
would have no more worries.

Sutra T. 16C11

World Honored One, the poor son then, hiring himself as a laborer here and there, unexpectedly arrived at his father's house. Standing by the gate, he saw his father seated on a Lion-seat. His feet were resting on a jeweled footstool, and he was reverently surrounded by Brahmans, Kshatriyas, and laypeople. Necklaces of real pearls, their value in the millions, adorned his body. Attendants and servants, holding white whisks, waited on him right and left. Above him was a jeweled canopy hung with flowers and pennants. Fragrant water was sprinkled on the ground, and expensive flowers were scattered about. Precious objects were placed in rows, which were passed out and taken in on leaving and entering. Such were the adornments, and the majesty and authority of his awesome virtue. When the poor son saw his father, possessed of such great power, he was immediately afraid and regretted having come there. Secretly he thought, 'This is perhaps a king, or one equal to a king. This is no place for me to hire myself out. I'd better go to a poor village where there will be room for me to work and where I can easily obtain clothing and food. If I stay here any longer, I may be forced to work.' And with this thought, he quickly ran off.

Outline:

> > M2. Father and son see
> > one another.
> >
> > > N1. Son sees the
> > > father.

Commentary:

WORLD HONORED ONE, THE POOR SON THEN, HIRING HIMSELF AS A LABORER HERE AND THERE...The Buddha's disciples had run off. Those of the Great Vehicle disposition had run away into the three realms. There, they were forced to undergo the eight sufferings, and so they were looking for a way out, a path out of suffering. They ran here and there seeking a method to escape but couldn't find one.

UNEXPECTEDLY ARRIVED AT HIS FATHER'S HOUSE. After a while, when they had been to many places, they came in turn to the place where the Buddha lived, that is, the Land of Expedients with Residue and the Land of Adornment of Real Retribution. STANDING BY THE GATE, he saw that his father's house was beautifully adorned. He didn't dare stand in the middle of the gate, but only off to one side. This represents the Small Vehicle people who dwell in two extremes: one is emptiness and the other falseness. They don't stand in the Middle Way. HE SAW HIS FATHER AT A DISTANCE. Although he was far away, his son could still see him. This shows that the Small Vehicle people still had the Great Vehicle disposition. SEATED ON A LION-SEAT... The seat was carved with lions on it. This represents that the Buddha sits on the Dharma King's seat manifesting the ten thousand foot high Reward Body. HIS FEET WERE RESTING ON A JEWELED FOOTSTOOL...The jeweled footstool represents the Buddha's perfection of both wisdom and samadhi.

AND HE WAS REVERENTLY SURROUNDED BY BRAHMANS. Brahmans are those who cultivate pure conduct. Here, they represent the Bodhisattvas at the stage of Equal Enlightenment who were present in the Avatamsaka Assembly. KSHASTRIYAS are the ruling class. Here they represent the Bodhisattvas from the First to the Ninth Grounds present in the Avatamsaka Assembly. LAYPEOPLE refers to the other Bodhisattvas in the Avatamsaka Assembly. The Buddha was surrounded by these great Bodhisattvas.

NECKLACES OF REAL PEARLS represent the ultimate keeping of precepts, the Shurangama Samadhi, and all the various aspects of real mark wisdom, as well as the four methods of conversion and so on. THEIR VALUE IN THE MILLIONS means that the Buddhadharma is wonderful beyond description, past all reckoning. ADORNED HIS BODY. These Dharma jewels adorned his Dharma appearance, and the Great Bodhisattvas surrounded him. ATTENDANTS refers to Bodhisattvas who have certified to the fruit. SERVANTS refers to those still cultivating expedients and the Paramitas. HOLDING WHITE WHISKS... They are brushes, made perhaps of horsehair, and used like dusters. In the Forty-two Hands

there is the White Whisk Hand. WAITED ON HIM RIGHT AND
LEFT represents entering into the wisdom of emptiness and
brushing away the dust of the Four Dwellings:

1. dwelling in the love of views;

2. dwelling in the love of desire;

3. dwelling in the love of form;

4. dwelling in the love of the formless.

The left represents entering into the wisdom of the false
and brushing away the dust of "unknowing." "Right and
left" then refers to brushing away the dust of emptiness
and falseness (existence).

ABOVE HIM WAS A JEWELED CANOPY. The jeweled canopy
represents his real compassion, his great compassion heart.
HUNG WITH FLOWERS AND PENNANTS. The flowers represent the
four methods of conversion: giving, kind words, conduct
profitable to others, and similar work. There are three
kinds of giving: 1. The giving of wealth 2. The giving of
Dharma. 3. The giving of fearlessness. Kind words
means speaking with compassion, speaking gently and without harshness or temper. It means dealing with all living
beings by using compassion, kindness, sympathetic joy and
giving. Practice profitable to others means that you benefit other people. Similar work means that you are one of
their kind. PENNANTS represent spiritual powers. There
are six spiritual powers: 1. The heavenly eye. 2. The heavenly ear. 3. The knowledge of other's thoughts. 4. The

knowledge of past lives. 5. The cessation of outflows.
6. The complete spirit.

FRAGRANT WATER WAS SPRINKLED ON THE GROUND. The fragrant water is the water of Dharma. The water of Dharma
is sprinkled on the ground of the minds of the Great Vehicle Bodhisattvas, washing away all the dust of their
delusions. The water is also the water of Samadhi, which
is sprinkled on the scattered mind to "unscatter it."

EXPENSIVE FLOWERS WERE SCATTERED ABOUT. They were
scattered in profusion, exquisite and valuable. The Great
Vehicle Bodhisattvas have seven pure flowers. The flowers above represented the four methods of conversion.
These flowers represent the seven pure flowers:

1. the three groups of pure precepts;

2. the great Shurangama Samadhi;

3. real wisdom;

4. cutting off doubts about the two truths;

5. practicing the wrong path while
     penetrating the Buddha Path;

6. virtue of wisdom;

7. virtue of severing.

To gain samadhi, one must first keep the precepts. If
you have samadhi, then you can gain wisdom. If you don't
keep the precepts, you won't gain samadhi, and you will
never give rise to wisdom. Therefore, in cultivating the
Way, the precepts are the most important requirement.

There are five basic precepts: 1. No killing. 2. No stealing. 3. No sexual misconduct. 4. No false speech. 5. No taking of intoxicants. Some people say, "Killing and stealing should be prohibited. Sexual misconduct is a little harder, but that should also be prohibited. Lying is no good, so that should be prohibited. But drinking -- what problem is there with drinking? Why include that? The Buddha must have made a mistake when he set up that precept."

Do you think this person's reasoning is correct? It may seem to have some principle, but actually it's totally wrong. Intoxicants confuse the nature. Once you drink, say, although you may never think about murdering someone, you might. You might not steal ordinarily, but under the influence of intoxicants you might steal, or with your desire inflamed by the alcohol you might commit sexual misconduct. You might lie under the influence, too. You might be asked what precepts you had broken, and you'd answer, "I didn't break any!"

This reminds me of a story about the five precepts. There was a layman who took the five precepts and swore off drinking. He didn't drink for two or three years, until the urge hit him. He thought, "Killing, stealing, sexual misconduct, and lying are definitely to be avoided. But it's not going to make any difference if I drink a little wine." He went out and bought some wine and took it home. He was a little tipsy, looking around for some hors d'oeurves, when, quite accidentally, the neighbor's chicken ran right into the house. "Fried chicken!" he thought, forgetting all about the precept against killing. "A gift from god!" he thought. "Probably, because I have not had a drink in so long, God has forgiven me and given me this chicken." He cut off its head and poured boiling water over it to remove the feathers. Then he fried it 'till it was quite crispy. The more he ate, the better the chicken tasted and the sweeter the wine got. He got so carried away, he even ate the chicken bones! He was ninety percent drunk by this time, when the neighbor lady knocked on his door. "Did my chicken come this way?" she asked him.

He was in a tight spot, indeed, but he got himself out of it by lying "I didn't see no chicken!" By this time he had drunk the wine, killed, stolen, and lied. Even though the chicken ran over on its own, still he took it and ate it without the owner's permission, so it counts as stealing. So he had broken four of the five precepts already. Because he was drunk, lust rose up in him. "She's really pretty," he thought, as he locked the door. Then he raped her! Thus, he broke all five precepts, just because he broke the precept against intoxicants. So, you can't break that precept.

The great Shurangama Samadhi, the Solid Samadhi, is the second flower. In whatever you do, you must be firm

and solid. If you aren't, you won't be able to persevere or attain to any greatness. If you are firm and solid, you can persevere and attain great, endless samadhi.
The great Shurangama Samadhi can never be destroyed.
Nothing can destroy it; it surpasses all.

The third pure flower, real wisdom, is our original
wisdom inherent in everyone. No one lacks it. However,
we forget about it and fail to make use of it. We use
provisional wisdom instead, the wisdom of expedients,
which is false and unreal. It is wisdom of the world.
Real wisdom is transcendental wisdom. With it one can
penetrate the real mark of all dharmas; one can understand all dharmas.

The fourth pure flower is that of cutting off doubts
concerning the two truths. The two truths are the common
truth and the real truth. The common truth refers to attachment to all worldly marks. The real truth is the nature of the transcendental. One refers to the marks and
the other to the nature.

Neither of these two truths reaches the absolute.
They correspond to the first two of the three contemplations. The common truth is the truth of emptiness, and
the real truth is the truth of falseness. They do not
reach the level of the middle way, but fall into the two
extremes. Cutting off delusions concerning these two
truths, then, is the fourth pure flower. While delusions

concerning them remain, one is not pure. When the delusions are cut off, one is pure.

The fifth pure flower is that of practicing on the
wrong path, but penetrating to the Buddha path. Although
one is going down the wrong road, one still manages to
return to the Buddha path. In this case, one's cultivation is not in accord with the wonderful doctrine of the
Great Vehicle, with the proper path. Perhaps one cultivates the small vehicle dharmas, or dharmas of outside religions, or unbeneficial austerities.

The sixth pure flower is the virtue of wisdom. When
the virtue of wisdom is perfected, one clearly sees the
original nature. One recognizes the original nature, that
is, sees the original mind. One understands the mind and
sees the nature.

The seventh pure flower is the virtue of severing.
When this virtue is perfected, ignorance is broken, is
ended, not just for a time, but forever.

These are the seven pure flowers referred to in the
text by the phrase "and expensive flowers were scattered
about."

PRECIOUS OBJECTS WERE PLACED IN ROWS represents the
wonderful dharmas of the Great Vehicle. WHICH WERE PASSED
OUT AND TAKEN IN ON LEAVING AND ENTERING. Real wisdom
was taken in. Passed out means that he went to transform
those with affinities. Taken in means those of the Two

Vehicles were attracted. Passed out means they were given the Great Vehicle Dharmas. SUCH WERE THE VARIOUS ADORNMENTS, as above mentioned, AND THE MAJESTY OF HIS AWESOME VIRTUE. This represents the limitlessness of his spiritual powers, the sea-like limitlessness of his thirty-two marks and eighty characteristics. These various marks, like the sea, are extermely majestic and awesome.

WHEN THE POOR SON SAW HIS FATHER...When those of the Small Vehicle saw the Buddha... They had run outside and didn't know the real method for cultivation. They ran all over, back and forth. When they returned, they saw the Buddha. POSSESSED OF SUCH GREAT POWER AND AUTHORITY...His great power represents the greatness of his wisdom. "Great authority" represents the greatness of his spiritual powers. They saw the Buddha's wisdom and spiritual powers were so great HE WAS IMMEDIATELY AFRAID. Upon seeing the Buddha's marks and characteristics of such adorned majesty, truly a body with sea-like marks, those of the small vehicle were afraid. Why? They had never seen anything so wonderful before. These marks surpassed those of the gods! So they were afraid. They thought, "Probably it's a demon king." AND REGRETTED HAVING COME THERE..."How did I get here?" SECRETLY HE THOUGHT, "THIS IS PERHAPS A KING OR ONE EQUAL TO A KING." "King" here does not refer to the king of a country nor does it refer to the Great Brahma Heaven King. It refers to the demon king. He was like Shariputra, who thought, "Could this be a demon come to disturb my mind?" Shariputra, with all his great wisdom, had some doubts. Now the poor son, who couldn't hold a candle to Shariputra as far as wisdom goes, thought this was a demon king or one of the demon's retinue that is, the demon's children and grandchildren. "THIS IS NO PLACE FOR ME TO HIRE MYSELF OUT. This is no place for me to cultivate. This is no place to make money. If I cultivate here, I won't get enlightened, I won't get any advantages. I'D BETTER GO TO A POOR VILLAGE WHERE THERE WILL BE ROOM FOR ME TO WORK. I'd be better off on the other side of the tracks, actually." This means he'd be better off cultivating the Two Vehicles. "I can work at my cultivation there. AND WHERE I CAN EASILY OBTAIN CLOTHING, the clothing of the aids of the Path, and the FOOD of the Proper Path. I'd be better off cultivating there.

"IF I STAY HERE ANY LONGER...If I wait around for very long I MAY BE FORCED TO WORK. I will be made to cultivate the Great Vehicle Dharma. I can't cultivate the Great Vehicle Dharma! You can't make me cultivate it, either! You can't force me, by gosh!" AND WITH THIS THOUGHT, this secret thought, HE QUICKLY RAN OFF. He thought that the Great Vehicle Dharma was too difficult to cultivate. The Great Vehicle Bodhisattvas must enter birth and death. Those of the Two Vehicles are afraid of birth and death. Those of the Great Vehicle roam and sport in birth and

death, purifying the Buddhalands, while teaching and
transforming living beings. They don't change and yet
accord with conditions. They accord with conditions and
yet do not change. They enter birth and death, and yet
they are not subject to birth and death. They abide in
the dust of the common world and yet transcend the dust
of the common world. That's the realm of the Great Vehicle. The people of the Two Vehicles find this terrify-
ing. "Gees! I'm not doing that! I can't cultivate that
Dharma." They look upon themselves as about as big as a
mote of dust. They aren't like the Bodhisattvas who en-
compass all of existence. Because followers of the two
vehicles' state is so small, they are afraid and quickly
run off. Where do they run to? To the small vehicle.

Sutra: T. 16c22
Then the wealthy elder, seated on the
Lion-seat, seeing his son, recognized him and
his heart rejoiced greatly, as he thought, "I
now have someone to whom I can bequeath
my wealth and treasuries. I have constantly been mindful of my son, but had no way
of seeing him. Then, all of a sudden, he came
on his own, and my wish has been fulfilled.
Although I am old and decrepit I still longed
for him with regret."

Outline:

N2. The father

sees the son.

Commentary:

THEN THE WEALTHY ELDER, the Buddha, SEATED ON THE LION-SEAT, the seat of the Dharma King, SEEING HIS SON, RECOGNIZED HIM. As soon as the Buddha saw those of the Two Vehicles, he recognized them. He said, "Although now they are living beings of the Two Vehicles, in the past I have taught them the principles of the Great Vehicle; consequently, they have the seeds of the Great Vehicle within them." Thus, he recognized them, AND HIS HEART REJOICED GREATLY. He was very, very happy, because the Buddha's vows are fulfilled when living beings are saved. AS HE THOUGHT, "I NOW HAVE SOMEONE TO WHOM I CAN BEQUEATH MY WEALTH AND TREASURIES. My wealth of Dharma and the treasuries of all the Dhyanas and liberations are limitless, the thirty-seven aids to the path, the six perfections, and the ten thousand practices, the four truths and the twelve links--all these Dharma treasures -- now there is someone to inherit them. I HAVE CONSTANTLY BEEN MINDFUL OF MY SON, thinking of those living beings of the Two Vehicles, BUT HAD NO WAY OF SEEING HIM. They were too far away; I couldn't see them. THEN, ALL OF A SUDDEN, HE CAME ON HIS OWN. They returned from the small vehicle and went to the Great Vehicle. AND MY WISH HAS BEEN FULFILLED. This is exactly as I wished it would be. ALTHOUGH I AM OLD AND DECREPIT, very old and about to enter Nirvana, I STILL LONGED FOR HIM WITH REGRET. I regretted that those of the Two Vehicles hadn't been crossed over. Now that those of the Two Vehicles have come, I can fulfill my dearest wish.

Sutra T.16c25

He then sent attendants to follow him and bring him back. Thereupon, the servants quickly apprehended him. The poor son in alarm shouted in resentment, "I have committed no offense. Why have I been seized?" The servants, with even greater haste, grabbed him and dragged him back. The poor son thought to himself, "I am blameless and yet have been imprisoned. This surely means that I will die," and, even more frightened, he fainted and fell to the ground.

The father saw his son from afar and said to the servant, "I do not need this person. Do not force him to come along. Sprinkle cold water on his face to bring him to, but do not speak further with him" Why was this? The father knew that his son's resolve and will were inferior and lowly, and that his own nobility was a source of difficulty to his son. Therefore, although he was certain that this was his son, he expediently refrained from telling anyone, "This is my son." The servant said to the son, "I now set you free. You may go wherever you wish". The poor son was delighted, having gained what he had never had before. He rose from the ground and went to a poor village to seek clothing and food.

Outline:

M3. Going after the son.

N1. Sending people

after the son.

Commentary:

HE THEN SENT ATTENDANTS...Because he recognized the Two Vehicle people and saw that they had returned and were about to run off yet again, he sent Bodhisattvas, Knights of the Dharma body, to go teach and transform them. TO FOLLOW HIM AND BRING HIM BACK. He said, "Go cross them over and tell them to return." THE SERVANTS, the Bodhisattvas, QUICKLY APPREHENDED HIM. The Bodhisattvas were in a great hurry to teach and transform them; they went there and spoke the Great Vehicle Dharma to them straight away, saying, "Hurry up and practice the Bodhisattva Path! The Bodhisattva Path is the Way to realization of Buddhahood." "Apprehended" him means that he spoke praises of the Great Vehicle Dharma hoping to cross them over.

THE POOR SON, IN ALARM...The people of the Two Vehicles had never before heard the Great Vehicle Dharma. They had spent their whole lives studying the Small Vehicle. Naturally, they were frightened. "Is there such a Dharma?" they wondered. "No..."

AND SHOUTED IN RESENTMENT. They had doubts about this Dharma door and felt resentment, because they felt unable to cultivate it themselves. "I HAVE COMMITTED NO OFFENSE.

I don't want to cultivate the Great Vehicle Dharma. Why
are you trying to force me into it? WHY HAVE I BEEN
SEIZED?"

THE SERVANTS, WITH EVEN GREATER HASTE, GRASPED HIM
AND DRAGGED HIM BACK. The more they didn't want to cultivate it, the more they insisted that they do. "No way.
You absolutely must cultivate the Great Vehicle Dharma and
return from the small towards the great. If you don't
cultivate the Great Vehicle Dharma, how can you become a
Buddha? Don't be so unreasonable. Hurry up and cultivate
the Great Vehicle." The more they didn't want to listen,
the more they forced them to listen. They more they tried
to get them to listen, the less they wanted to listen, and
they grew fearful.

The more the servants tried to drag him back, the
more frightened he became. "What's going on here?" he
thought. "I'm being taken under false pretenses. If you
really wanted me to cultivate, why would you be so impa-
tient and rash about it?"

THE POOR SON THOUGHT TO HIMSELF, "I AM BLAMELESS."
"I never wanted to cultivate this Dharma. Why are you trying to make me cultivate it now? Why are you taking me
into custody like this? AND YET HAVE BEEN IMPRISONED. I
should be able to cultivate whatever Dharma I want to. Why
are you trying to force me to cultivate your Dharma? THIS
SURELY MEANS THAT I WILL DIE." If I cultivate your Dharma,

it's all over for me. I'll die. That is, I won't realize
the Way." AND, EVEN MORE FRIGHTENED...The more they tried
to cross him over, the more frightened he became. HE
FAINTED AND FELL TO THE GROUND. He was scared to death!

THE FATHER, the Buddha, SAW HIS SON, those of the
Two Vehicles, FROM AFAR, that is, scared to death. "From
afar" means that he saw that those of the Two Vehicles refused the teaching of the Bodhisattvas. He then decided
to use an expedient device. He said to his servant, AND
SAID TO THE SERVANT, "I DO NOT NEED THIS PERSON." Don't
speak the Dharma to him. Don't try to talk him into it
saying, "The Buddhadharma is great. It's the most wonderful. You can end birth and death and gain wisdom if you
study it." Since he doesn't know anything at all about
it, he simply thinks, "What's he talking about? What's
'ending birth and death?' What do you mean, 'gain wisdom?'" If you tell him too much, he just runs away. You
have to be able to see what people like. So, today one
disciple first gave her son a piece of candy. She didn't
worry about whether or not he believed in the Buddhadharma. First give them something sweet. Then, ever after-
ward they will remember the Buddhist Lecture Hall as being sweet, and it will be a pleasant memory. If you give
them bitter-melon as soon as they get here, they won't
like it. If you tell them, "It's really bitter here. It's
very difficult to cultivate the Way," they won't want to

cultivate. They won't want the bitterness. I believe that if some of my disciples had known how hard it was here when they first came--you have to get up early, and you get to bed late--they would have run off long ago for sure. But they have gained a taste for cultivation and now, even though they may think about running off, still they want to give it a try.

I have one disciple who wants to leave home, but he has lied to me several times. People said to me that I should not allow him to leave home, because in the future if he didn't follow the precepts it would be bad. It would be best just to tell him to leave. I thought it over and people all come to understanding from having not understood. Now, he wants to cultivate the Way, and this is not an easy matter. In America, this heavenly place, no one wants to fall into the hells. Those who have left home do not eat well, their living arrangements are not the best, and most people would consider this hell. But, this hell is a hell for ending suffering. It's not like the Avichi hells which have no end. So, we will let him have another chance to cultivate the Way. In Buddhism one must be compassionate. We'll see how it goes, give it a try.

"I DO NOT NEED THIS PERSON. DO NOT FORCE HIM TO COME ALONG." Don't force him to cultivate the Great Vehicle Buddhadharma. Wait a while.

"SPRINKLE COLD WATER ON HIS FACE TO BRING HIM TO, BUT DO NOT SPEAK FURTHER WITH HIM." He was so frightened that he fainted on the spot. Now, the cold water on his face brought the three hun and seven p'ai back and revived him once again. This means that he just waited, and the son thought it over and understood by himself. I am waiting now, too.

WHY WAS THIS? THE FATHER KNEW THAT HIS SON'S RESOLVE AND WILL WERE INFERIOR AND LOWLY, AND THAT HIS OWN NOBIL- ITY WAS A SOURCE OF DIFFICULTY TO HIS SON. The poor son was afraid of the Great Vehicle Buddhadharma so he passed out, collapsing on the ground. The servant sprinkled cold water on his face. This represents the water of the tea- ching of the Four Holy Truths. The teaching of the Four Truths "brought him to," that is, led him to cultivate and certify to the fruit.

"The father knew that his son's -- the Buddha knew that those of the Small Vehicle's -- resolve and will were inferior and lowly." They didn't have much sense. Be- cause their dispositions inclined to the Small Vehicle, one couldn't teach them the Great Vehicle Buddhadharma. "And that his own nobility"--the Buddha knew that he him- self was powerful; his Dharmabody pervades all places. Both his Reward and Response Bodies are very noble and esteemed--"was a source of difficulty to his son..." It's very hard for those of the Small Vehicle to believe in.

It's very hard to belive in.

THEREFORE, ALTHOUGH HE WAS CERTAIN THAT THIS WAS HIS SON. The Buddha, observing the potentials and the causal conditions, knew that these living beings had already, during the time of twenty-million Buddhas been taught and transformed, thus acquiring the seeds of the Great Vehicle. Therefore, he knew for sure they were sons of the Buddha. HE EXPEDIENTLY REFRAINED FROM TELLING ANYONE, "THIS IS MY SON." Since they couldn't accept the Great Vehicle Dharma, he used the expedient device dharma doors to teach and transform those of the Small Vehicle. "He refrained from telling anyone," means that, in this present incarnation, when teaching the Four Truths, the Twelve Links, and so on, from the Agama to the Prajna teachings, he never told anyone that those of the Two Vehicles could become Buddhas. He never said, "This is my son," as he did in the Dharma Flower Assembly when he told Shariputra that in the future he would be a Buddha by the name of Flower Light. The Buddha never said that the Sound Hearers were the Buddha's sons. He only said that of the Bodhisattvas.

THE SERVANT SAID TO THE SON.. The servant refers to the Buddha's wisdom, to the Buddha's teaching, and also to the Bodhisattvas.

"I NOW SET YOU FREE." I am not going to force you to cultivate the Great Vehicle. "YOU MAY GO WHEREVER YOU

WISH. Do what you like. If you want to cultivate the Small Vehicle, go ahead, as you please. I won't insist on teaching you the Great Vehicle Dharma."

THE POOR SON WAS DELIGHTED. Those of the Small Vehicle thought, "We get to do whatever we want! We can keep cultivating the Small Vehicle." They had never been so happy. HAVING GAINED WHAT HE HAD NEVER HAD BEFORE. HE ROSE FROM THE GROUND. He had fainted and was still lying on the ground. Now, having been revived with cold water, he rose. He had thought to quit cultivating, but now he resolved to continue cultivating his Small Vehicle dharmas. AND WENT TO A POOR VILLAGE TO SEEK CLOTHING AND FOOD. He went to a poverty stricken village, that is, to the realm of the Two Vehicles, to cultivate the small vehicle path, to seek the clothing of the Proper Dharma and the food of the Aids to the Path.

Sutra: T. 17 a 7

Then the elder, wishing to induce his son, set up an expedient and secretly sent two people, haggard and undignified in appearance, saying to them, "You may go there and gently speak to that poor one. Tell him there is a place for him to work here where he can earn twice as much. If he agrees, bring him back and put him to work. If he asks what he is to do, tell him, 'You are being hired to sweep out dung. We two will work along with you.'"

Outline:

> > N2. Sending two people af-
> > ter the son.
> > > O1. The instruction.
> > > > P1. Suitability of
> > > > three carts.

Commentary:

Those of the Two Vehicles on the Position of Seeing
the Way (first stage arhatship) and the Position of Cultivating the Way (second and third stage arhatship), were
in the poverty stricken village. THEN THE ELDER, WISHING
TO INDUCE HIS SON...The Buddha was just about to do this;
he was developing a plan and contemplating the potential
conditions in order to teach and transform these living
beings. He was going to use a clever expedient method to
induce his son, and so he SET UP AN EXPEDIENT AND SECRET-
LY SENT TWO PEOPLE...What does this mean? Who are these
two people? They are Bodhisattvas who have transformed
themselves into Sound Hearers and Conditioned Enlightened
Ones. In terms of the Dharma, the Teaching, we would say
that they are the Four Truths and the Twelve Links.

"Secretly sent" according to the Teaching, represents the "Half Teaching" and the "Full Teaching." The
Full Teaching is The Lotus Sutra, the Perfect Teaching.
The Storehouse Teaching and the Pervasive Teaching are
the "Half Teaching." The Full Teaching is represented by

the word "secretly." The Half Teaching is represented by
the word "sent."

To explain it according to the people, "secretly"
means that inwardly they practiced the Bodhisattva Path,
but outside they manifested as Sound Hearers "sent" to
induce living beings.

According to the two teachings, provisional and
real, the word "secretly" represents the real teaching;
the word "sent" represents the provisional teaching. The
Bodhisattvas are sent in secret; as Sound Hearers they
are sent to do the work.

The Bodhisattvas transform into Sound Hearers HAGGARD
IN APPEARANCE AND UNDIGNIFIED...Those of the Small Vehicle
do not cultivate fine marks. What do they do? They cultivate the dharmas of suffering, emptiness, impermanence,
impurity, and no self. They think, "Everything's really
suffering. It's incredible. I'd better cultivate, hey!
There's nothing to be attached to. It's all empty--mean-
ingless! The twelve links, all dharmas, are impermanent.
What is there to cling to? There is no self; attachments
must be broken. The world of the five turbidities is impure; it's filthy, indeed. The body is dirty--everything
is unclean." They cultivate in order to attain bliss,
permanence, true self, and purity. They awaken to the
principle of one-sided emptiness. They haven't been enlightened to the principle of the middle way, so they

don't cultivate the thirty-two marks and eighty minor
characteristics of the Buddha. Their appearance is haggard. If one manifested the ten thousand foot Nishyanda
body of the Buddha, they wouldn't believe in it. So the
Bodhisattvas disguise themselves as haggard-looking Sound
Hearers.

"Undignified" means they had no awesome virtue. They
do not have the Ten Powers or the Four Fearlessnesses.
Without the Ten Powers and the Four Fearlessnesses, the
Bodhisattvas were the same as those of the Two Vehicles.
"YOU MAY GO THERE AND GENTLY SPEAK TO THAT POOR ONE." So the
Buddha had the Bodhisattvas disguise themselves as poor
folks, too, as those of the Two Vehicles. Then he sent
them to the poor village to speak to the poor person, gently. They shouldn't be nervous and try to drag him back
like they did before. They should take their time and not
speak the Great Vehicle Dharma to them right away. TELL
HIM THERE IS A PLACE FOR HIM TO WORK HERE, a place for him
to cultivate the Way. This means that there was a place
for him to cultivate the position of seeing the Way, First
Stage Arhatship, and the position of cultivating the Way,
the Second and Third Stages of Arhatship. A place to
work means a place to cut off their delusions of views
and thought. The Bodhisattvas will gradually teach him
to cut off his delusions of views and thoughts and give
him a Position of Seeing the Way and of Cultivating the

Way.

Now, those of outside ways can subdue their delusions, thereby gaining birth in the form and formless realm heavens. They talk about being born in Paradise, but they have only subdued their delusions; they have not cut them off. Although they may be born in the heavens, they still have not ended birth and death; they have not escaped the Three Realms in the Burning House.

WHERE HE CAN EARN TWICE AS MUCH. This means he can certify to the Fourth Fruit of Arhatship. When they teach him the Four Truths and the Twelve Links and he cultivates according to them, he can end birth and death; he can certify to the Fourth Fruit, thus transcending the Three Realms and the Five Elements. By ending birth and death, he can "earn twice as much."

IF HE AGREES, BRING HIM BACK AND PUT HIM TO WORK. "Agrees" means if that potential is there and he can be saved, then save him. If he can't be saved, then stop. Bring him back and put him to work cultivating the Way.

IF HE ASKS WHAT HE IS TO DO, TELL HIM, 'YOU ARE BE-ING HIRED TO SWEEP OUT THE DUNG.' This just means cleaning out the toilets. What are the toilets? They are an analogy for the first two of the Four Holy Truths: suffering and origination, and also for casting out the delusions of views and of thought. It also refers to casting out the "dung" of ignorance. Those of the Two Vehicles cultivate suffering and emptiness, but they do not care about purifying the Buddhalands. They merely cast out the dung and do not care to purify the Buddhalands and bring living beings to accomplishment. They don't care to practice the Bodhisattva path, and so they simply sweep out the dung. That's what they are hired to do.

WE TWO WILL WORK ALONG WITH YOU. These two refers to the Small and Great Vehicles side by side. The Great Vehicle is leading the Small Vehicle and the Small Vehicle is turning towards the Great Vehicle. This refers to those of provisional potentials and those of real potentials cultivating together, that is, the Bodhisattvas and Sound Hearers working together.

Sutra: T.17a11
Then the two servants sought out the poor son, and when they found him, they told him the above matter in detail.

Outline:

> P2. Knowing son's
> former thoughts.
> P3. Praising the
> three carts.

Commentary:

THEN THE TWO SERVANTS SOUGHT OUT THE POOR SON, AND WHEN THEY FOUND HIM. The Buddha sent the two off with instructions. Once they were in their disguises, they sought

out the poor son, the small vehicle person. Then they
talked with him, chatting about the Small Vehicle dharma
AND TOLD HIM THE ABOVE MATTER IN DETAIL.

Sutra: T. 17a12

At that time the poor son first took his salary and then joined them in sweeping away the dung. When the father saw his son, he felt pity and amazement.

Outline:

> P4. Inducing resolve
> to escape the burn-
> ing house.

Commentary:

The poor son probably had been cheated before, and so
he wanted to be paid in advance. AT THAT TIME THE POOR SON
FIRST TOOK HIS SALARY AND THEN JOINED THEM IN SWEEPING AWAY
THE DUNG. What does this mean? This means that he asked
first of all, "If I cultivate, what benefits will I obtain?
You want me to cultivate the Four Truths and the Twelve
Links. What's in it for me?" He insisted on taking his
wages first, before joining the two in sweeping away the
filth. "Sweeping away the dung" means getting rid of the
filth of the Truth of Suffering and of Origination. It
also means getting rid of the dung of the delusions of
views and thought.

WHEN THE FATHER SAW HIS SON... When the Buddha saw

those of the Two Vehicles HE FELT PITY, he thought they were pitiful. "I have the Dharma Jewel of the Great Vehicle. Why don't you cultivate it. Why do you insist on cultivating the fruit of the Small Vehicle? It's pathetic. AND AMAZEMENT... They don't seek the Great Vehicle Buddhadharma. This is really very strange. Why do they insist on cultivating the Small Vehicle Dharma? Wierd."

The "salary" refers to the wages within The Dharma Flower Sutra. When we speak of the worth of The Dharma Flower Sutra, it is inconceivable, subtle, and wonderful, indeed. This reminds me of a story about a person who used to recite The Lotus Sutra. This took place during the Chin Dynasty in China. There was a Dharma Master named T'an-i. This Dharma Master wasn't a person. He was a pheasant. Where did he come from? Previously, in Yü-hang there was a Dharma Master named Fa-chih. He specialized in lecturing on The Lotus Sutra. Once, a pheasant came to listen to his lectures. The pheasant came to all his lectures for seven years! Then it died. Someone is thinking, "Listening to Sutras must not be that good. The pheasant listened to death! Let's not Listen." Well, the pheasant may have died, but that very night, Dharma Master Fa-chih had a dream in which he saw a young boy who spoke to him saying, "I am that pheasant who used to come to your Sutra lectures. Now, because of the power of listening to The Lotus Sutra, I won't be born again as

a pheasant; I will be born as a person. I will be born
in the house of a Mr. Wong at the foot of the mountain tomorrow, and in the future I plan to leave home under you.
About three or four years later, Mr. Wong asked Dharma Master Fa-chih to lunch, and as soon as he went in the door
the boy said, "My Dharma Master has come!" Because he had
had a dream, he knew that the boy was a pheasant. He said
to the boy's father, "Your son is a pheasant," and he
ripped the boy's shirt off his back, and sure enough, there
were three feathers on his back! That was proof. Mr. Wong
said, "Oh, so he is a pheasant. Now he can cultivate."
And when the boy was seven years old, he allowed him to
leave home. He then concentrated on reciting The Lotus
Sutra and built a hut for cultivation, called the Dharma
Flower Cottage, in which he recited the Sutra for about
ten years. One day a woman came. She was carrying a bas-
ket with a little white pig and garlic bulbs in it. She
was wearing brightly colored clothes, like a woman who
doesn't follow the rules. She wanted to stay overnight
at the cottage. She had been gathering medicinal herbs
in the mountains all day. She hadn't found any and was
afraid of the tigers and other wild beasts that roamed
those mountains, and so she insisted on staying. Dharma
Master T'an-I refused. "I can't allow a woman to stay
here. Go find some other place." There wasn't any other
place, however, and she was bound and determined to stay

with him. There was no way he could get rid of her. So
he let her stay on a heap of straw. That night something
very strange happened, too. In the middle of the night
the woman started crying and complaining that her stomach
hurt. She insisted that he come and massage her stomach.
What do you think he did in the face of such a karmic ob-
stacle? He wrapped his staff in a cloth and, from a great
distance, he rubbed her stomach with the staff. That way
he didn't have to touch her. After a bit she felt better.
However, the next day, at dawn, her bright colored clothes
rose up into space and turned into a five-colored cloud.
Her little white pig turned into an elephant. The two
cloves of garlic turned into two white lotuses upon which
her feet rested. She spoke to him from her place in
space saying, "Your cultivation isn't bad. I am Saman-
tabahadra Bodhisattva. In a few days you are due to enter my Dharma Assembly, and so I decided to test you out
ahead of time. Your mind of the Way isn't bad at all;
it's quite solid. You have passed my test, then, and in
the future you will be one of my retinue." Then empty
space was filled with light and fragrance. The Emperor
saw it and later built Dharma Flower Monastery there.

Think of it, a pheasant heard The Dharma Flower Sutra and obtained such a great response. If we people
hear The Dharma Flower Sutra, we should attain an even
greater response.

During the time of Liang Wu-ti in China, there was a Bhikshuni by the name of Tao-chi. Her other name was Tsung-ch'ih. She was Bodhidharma's disciple. She lived alone in a hut and recited The Dharma Flower Sutra exclusively. That's what she did all her life. When she died, they buried her beside her little hut. After seven or eight years a blue lotus grew up out of her grave. The Emperor found out about this. When he saw it, he ordered the grave opened, so they could see where the blue lotus was growing from. They found it was growing from her mouth. This is an inconceivable state. Why did the blue lotus grow out of her mouth? Because, when she was alive, she recited The Lotus Sutra. This is proof of the inconceivability of reciting The Dharma Flower Sutra.

There was also a Bhikshuni named Hua-shou (flower hands). She kept the precepts very purely and never broke them. She also recited The Dharma Flower Sutra. Every time she recited the Sutra, a lotus would appear on the lines of her hand. Her entire hands became covered with these lotuses, as she recited the Sutra all her life. The Emperor asked her to visit him, and when he saw all the lotuses on her hands he gave her the name "Flower Hands."

These are some of the inconceivable things that have happened in China as a result of reciting The Dharma Flower Sutra. To say nothing of hearing the entire Sutra explained, even to hear the name means that one has great good roots.

You say, "Well, then, do we who are listening to it now have good roots?"

Of course! If you didn't have good roots you would not even be able to get in the door. Or you might get in, but you would immediately want to run. You wouldn't be able to stay very long. It's not that simple. The worth of The Dharma Flower Sutra is inconceivable. This present lecture series on The Dharma Flower Sutra is also inconceivable.

Another thing: There was also a Dharma Master named Fa-yün who specialized in lecturing on The Dharma Flower Sutra. When he did so, he was wonderfully eloquent and intelligent. He lectured extremely well. Another Dharma Master made a vow that in every life he would be just like this Dharma Master, that he would look the same and have the same eloquence and vow power. That night he had a dream in which someone said, "Don't think it's so easy to be like him. He was lecturing on the Sutra even at the time of the Buddha Sun-Moon-Lamp Brightness. This isn't new for him. That's why he's so incredibly good at it. If you want to be like him, it will have to be done gradually." So the lecturing of this Sutra is Dharma which is hard to encounter. That's why I say that its worth is inconceivable.

Sutra: T. 17a14
Later, on another day, through a window, he saw his son at a distance . . .

Outline:

02. The intention.

P1. Provisional
wisdom's suita-
bility.

Commentary:

LATER, ON ANOTHER DAY... "Another" refers to those
of the Two Vehicles who take the doctrines of the Provisional Teaching as their own. They think the doctrines
of the Real Teaching belong to "another." "Another" represents the doctrine of the Real Teaching. "Day" could
also mean "time" or "wisdom." Relying on the wisdom of
the Real Teaching, the Buddha teaches all those with potential.

THROUGH A WINDOW... The door is at the center, and
the windows are off to either side. This means that one
looks from a one-sided view-point. Why? Was the Elder
sneaking looks at them? No. It was because, if the Buddha looked at them from the point of view of the middle
way, they would be afraid, fearing the Buddha's awesome
virtue. Thus, he stands on the side of one-sided emptiness, looking at those of the Two Vehicles.

HE SAW HIS SON AT A DISTANCE... A distance means
that because they are so small compared to the Great Vehicle, they seem very distant.

Sutra: T. 17 a 14
   ... thin, haggard, soiled with dung,
dirt, and filth.

Outline:

> P2. Knowing for
> a long time the
> son's delight in
> lesser dharmas.

Commentary:

THIN means that they had no wisdom. They had not
cultivated great wisdom and intelligence, so they were
thin. They were thin, also because they had not cultivated blessings. They did not, like the Buddha, cultivate
blessings and wisdom for three asamkheya aeons and perfect
the fine marks for another hundred aeons. That's why
they were so skinny.

HAGGARD means that, within the Three Realms they were
burned by the Five Skandhas. They were hassled by the
eight sufferings, as well.

DUNG is the afflictions of the Four Dwellings:

    1. the affliction of the dwelling in views
       and love;

    2. the affliction of the dwelling in desire
       and love;

    3. the affliction of the dwelling in form
       and love;

    4. the affliction of the dwelling in
       formlessness and love.

These four afflictions are the "dung."

DIRT refers to the affliction of ignorance.

SOILED with this FILTH of the afflictions of the Four Dwellings and the afflictions of ignorance; they haven't cut off their false thinking or stopped climbing on conditions. If you have false thinking and climb on conditions, that is being soiled with filth. Without them, you are pure. So, those who cultivate the Way should not borrow money. That's dirty. And you shouldn't have false thinking, hoping people will make offerings to you. If you do that, if you tell people to make offerings to you and you climb on conditions, that is dirty, it's being soiled with filth. Now do you understand? Real cultivators wouldn't care if they starved to death. So what? It's no problem. It's going to happen sooner or later anyway. Why look on it as so important? Why recite some song to get a god to come and help you out? Don't be af-

raid! Wei-t'ou Bodhisattva has made a vow that if someone is even 30% sincere in their cultivation they will
obtain 100% of a response. He will help you out. If you
don't cultivate, then, of course, there will be no response. If you have not the slightest bit of cultivation,
how can you expect a response? No matter how great or
small, you should apply some effort every day in cultivation.

What is cultivation? Bowing to the Buddha, reciting the Buddha's name, reading the Sutras, bowing to the
Sutras are all cultivation. In general, do not rational-
ize for yourself saying, "I've got to rest, take a nap.
Or perhaps I'll just sneak off for a break. That's the
best way." Don't do that, and you can be considered cultivating, and Wei-t'ou Bodhisattva will protect you. If
you just take breaks, that's not cultivating, and no one
will make offerings to you no matter how hard you try to
climb on conditions and soil yourself with that filth.

Once, I was without food. Originally, people made
offerings, but somebody tried to ruin my reputation and
told everyone not to make offerings to me. He told them
they shouldn't make offerings to me because I didn't cultivate and had no Way Virtue. He said he had the Way Virtue and that they should make offerings to him, not me.
The temple that had been making offerings to me suddenly
stopped. How could they make offerings to someone who

lacked Way Virtue? After a while, I was on the verge of starvation and so, stupid as I was, I thought, "If I starve to death, I starve to death. Let it be." Although I was, in fact, starving, I didn't tell anyone that I had no food. Wei-t'ou Bodhisattva got on the case and he appeared in a dream to a certain layperson, telling him to make offerings to me. I've told you about this before. So I know that Wei-t'ou Bodhisattva will certainly help you if you have a true mind to cultivate the Way, a mind which isn't even afraid of death. Don't worry that no one will make offerings to you.

Sutra: T.17 a 15

He then removed his necklace of beads, his soft upper garments, and his adornments and put on a coarse, worn out, and filthy robe, smeared himself with dirt and holding a dung shovel, looking frightful...

Outline:

P3. Knowing for a long time the necessity of praising the three carts.

Commentary:

HE THEN REMOVED HIS NECKLACE OF BEADS. The necklace

is an analogy for all the Buddha's dharmas, the precepts, samadhis, and wisdom, the dharanis--all the dharmas. He hid away his awesome and majestic appearance, so the text says, he "removed his necklace of beads."

HIS SOFT UPPER GARMENTS, the most expensive clothing. The Buddha's great, adorned body, has fine marks which are like the sea. The Buddha has limitless marks, like the sea. This refers to the thirty-two marks and the eighty minor characteristics. He is adorned with awesome virtue. Now, he has hid away this body. Why? Because those of the Two Vehicles don't recognize the Buddha. The Buddha is basically their father, but they do not admit this, because he is too wealthy, and they are so terribly poor. If the Buddha tried to cross them over with this majestic body, they would grow frightened. Why? Because those of the lesser vehicle haven't ever seen such a venerable body adorned with such marks. That's why the Buddha removes the necklace of beads and the soft upper garments AND HIS ADORNMENTS AND PUT ON A COARSE... What is meant by "coarse?" The Buddha hid away his ten thousand foot high <u>nishyana</u> body and manifested the six foot high body of an old Bhikshu, which looked more or less the same as that of everyone else.

WORN OUT... Worn out refers to the small vehicle dharma's patience of production and patience of dharmas.

FILTHY ROBE means that it was badly stained.

SMEARED HIMSELF WITH DIRT... The outflows of conditioned existence are unclean. Conditioned dharmas and the causes of outflows are the dirt. Affliction, also is like dirt and dust.

AND HOLDING A DUNG SHOVEL IN HIS RIGHT HAND... The right hand represents the use of expedient dharmas to teach and transform those of the Small Vehicle. The dung shovel refers to the Dharma-door breaking through the delusions of views and thought, that is, getting rid of the dung. The Buddha uses this dharma to cut off delusions of views and thought and the delusions of ignorance and thereby become a Buddha. He uses this kind of Dharma to teach all living beings. He teaches those of the small vehicle to rely upon this method to cut off their delusions and accomplish the Buddha Path. This is represented by "holding a dung shovel."

LOOKING FRIGHTFUL... He appears in the guise of one of the small vehicle, fearing birth and death. The Bodhisattva ends birth and death while in the midst of birth and death. Bodhisattvas are not afraid of suffering, nor are they afraid of birth and death. Those of the Two Vehicles are afraid of both birth and death. They are afraid of impermanence and afraid of suffering. Thus, the Buddha manifests as if he were afraid of birth and death, impermanence, and suffering, too.

This also represents the Buddha's enduring the retribution of the headaches and of horse feed.

When the Buddha was on the causal ground, a long, long time ago, in his country there was a drought. Since there was nothing else to eat, people started eating fish. A very large fish was caught and brought up on the shore. Shakyamuni Buddha was then just a child. He picked up the fish and hit it over the head twice. So, even after he had become a Buddha, he sometimes had headaches.

Another time, in a former life, while cultivating, he saw a Bhikshu begging for alms, and he thought, "That Bhikshu can darned well eat horse feed! Why do people give him such tasty things to eat?" Because when he was on the causal ground he said that one sentence, when he became a Buddha the following event took place: The Buddha went to another country to spend the rainy season. The king had said he would make offerings to him, but when the Buddha got there, the king reneged. "Just give these Bhikshus horse feed!" he said, and for three months the Sangha ate horse feed.

In spite of his great awesome virtue, even the Buddha had to suffer retribution when it manifested. That's what the text means by "looking frightful." It is discussing the doctrine of cause and effect. It is said:

Plant a good cause, reap a good effect.

Plant an evil cause, reap an evil effect.

The causes you planted in your former lives determine the

effects you now undergo. Shakyamuni Buddha, long ago, hit the fish twice, and over five hundred people ate its flesh. Thus, after he became a Buddha, he often had headaches.

There was also the incident when the Great King Crystal tried to wipe out the Shakyan clan. He was King of India, and he wanted to kill every one of them. The Shakyan clan was, in fact, composed of those very people who, in the past, had eaten that fish. King Crystal was formerly that fish! Since they had eaten his flesh, he wanted to drink their blood. He was determined to kill them all. The Buddha, although he had become a Buddha and possessed all the spiritual powers, wonderful as they are, couldn't save his kinsfolk.

Mahamaudgalyayana, however, couldn't stand this, and he tried to use his spiritual powers to save them. The Buddha couldn't save them because it was fixed retribution, determined by former causes and effects. Madgalyayana didn't know the cause and effect. He was an Arhat, and he could only see into the past as far back as eighty thousand great aeons. He thought, "My teacher's clansfolk are going to be killed by the King. I must manifest my spiritual powers and save them!" Everyone knows that he was number one when it came to spiritual penetrations. Well, he recited a mantra and put five hundred members of the Shakyan clan into his begging bowl and sent it up into empty space. "There's no way King Crystal can kill them now," he thought. When King Crystal had finished off the Shakyan clan, Maudgalyayana brought the bowl down again. Much to his dismay, he found the five hundred Shakyans he had saved had turned into a sea of blood. There was no life there at all. Maudgalyayana asked the Buddha, "With my power, why couldn't I rescue them?"

The Buddha told him, "There's no way to avoid the workings of cause and effect. If they could be avoided, I would have saved them myself. I wouldn't have needed to wait for you to save them."

Cause and effect is difficult to escape. Causes you planted in former lives take their toll in this present life; one must undergo the retribution.

As a good example of cause and effect, take a look at at what happened to National Master Wu-ta. (For details, see The Dharma Flower Sutra, Volume I, pp. 26-28.) It was just his one thought of arrogance, "Here I am, sitting on the beautiful carved chair given to me by the Emperor. I must be the highest Dharma Master there is!" that brought all his karmic obstacles down on him again.

When one thought of arrogance arises,

Eighty-four thousand karmic obstacles arrive.
His karma of resentment dated all the way back to the Han Dynasty, when he had murdered a man out of jealousy. La-ter, repenting, he left home. While he was being a cons-

cientious cultivator, and repenting of his former evil deeds, his obstacles had to stay away. But once he got arrogant, the Dharma Protectors, who had been fending of his ghost, ran away, "He's so arrogant. What a creep!" they thought. "We're not going to protect you." Since Wei-t'ou left him, the ghost came back, and his leg broke out with a sore which looked just like a human face. It could even talk! All day long it asked for meat to eat. It was a lot of trouble, but it all came from that one arrogant thought.

Sutra : T17a17
. . . he addressed his workers, saying, "All of you, work hard! Do not be lax." By this device he draws near to his son, to whom he later says, " Hey, my boy! You should stay here and work. Don't go elsewhere. I will increase your wages. Whatever you need, be it pots, utensils, rice, flour, salt or vinegar or other such things, don't trouble yourself about it. I also have an old, worn-out servant you can have if you need him. So put your mind at rest. I am like your father, so have no more worries. Why? I am very old, and you are young and strong. Whenever you are working, you are never deceitful, remiss, angry, hateful, or grumbling. I have never seen you commit such evils as I have the other workers. From now on you shall be just like my own son."

Just then the elder gave him a name, calling him his son. The poor son, although delighted at his happening, still referred to himself as a lowly worker from outside. For this reason, for twenty years he was constantly kept at work sweeping away dung.

Outline:

> P4. Knowing his wish
> to receive and prac-
> tice.

Commentary:

HE SPOKE TO HIS WORKERS, SAYING... "Workers" are those he employs. This is an analogy for the Dharma of the Four Applications of Mindfulness. "Speaking to his workers" means that he taught the Four Applications of Mindfulness. They are: mindfulness with regard to the 1) body; 2) feelings; 3) thoughts; and, 4) dharmas.

First of all, one contemplates the body as impure. Most people think that their bodies are the most important thing. For this reason, they forget about their self natures. Actually, the body is by no means the real self. You can say, "This _is_ my body." But you cannot say, "I _am_ my body." If you get attached and cling to your body, then you will daily grow stupider and more confused. You should understand that the body is not really you. It is _yours_,

因果經云有長者子名耶舍有大辯才
聰明智慧於中夜分見空中光明尋光
詣鹿野苑見佛三十二相八十種好禮
佛白言唯願世尊救濟於我佛言色受
想行識無常苦空無我汝知否答言實
是聞是語已得法眼淨成阿羅漢願求
出家佛言善來比丘即成沙門時即舍
父尋子耶舍至於佛所佛以神力隱其
即舍而為說法善男子色受想行識無
常苦空無我汝知否耶舍父聞已遠塵
離垢見於道跡如來問言何緣至此答
言尋子佛攝神力父子相見心大歡喜
佛即受三自歸為最初優婆塞又有耶
舍朋類五十長者子聞即出家共詣
佛所願求出家佛言色受想行識無常
苦空無我汝知否聞已滿盡意解佛言
善來比丘即成沙門是時始有五十六
阿羅漢佛告比丘汝等堪為世間作無
上福田宜各遊方教化以慈悲心度諸
眾生

Yashas, son of an Elder, takes refuge with the Buddha
(See The Amitabha Sutra, BTTS, 1974, p.64)

目連救母

孟蘭盆經云大目犍連始得六通欲度
父母報乳哺之恩即以道眼觀視世間
見其亡母生餓鬼中不見飲食皮骨連
立目連悲哀即以鉢盛飯往餉其母母
得鉢飯便以左手接鉢右手搏食食未
入口化成火炭遂不得食目連大叫悲
號涕泣馳還白佛具陳如此佛言汝母
罪根深結非汝一人力所奈何汝雖孝
順聲動天地天神地祇亦不能奈何當
須說救濟之法令一切難皆離憂苦當
於七月十五日為七世父母及現在父
母具飯百味五果汲灌盆器盡世甘美
以著盆中供養十方大德眾僧供養此
等自恣僧者若現在父母壽命百年無
病無一切苦惱之患乃至七世父母出
離三塗餓鬼之苦生人天中福樂無極
是佛弟子修孝順者應念念中常憶父
母年年七月十五日為作孟蘭盆施佛
及僧

Mahamaudgalyayana rescues his mother. (See p.872)

like a house which you live in for a while. You can't
say that your body is you. If you lived in a house, you
would say it was yours; you wouldn't say that it was you!
If you did, everyone would think you were pretty stupid.
Our bodies are like houses, too. We live in them and
take care of them for a while, but there is no need to
get so attached to them.

You should contemplate the body as impure. I have
lectured these many times before, but the more you hear
it, the more Bodhi seeds you plant. The body is filthy,
in fact. When you are alive, it oozes filth from nine
apertures. The eyes excrete matter, the nose and ears
do, too. There is saliva in the mouth. That's seven
apertures. Add the eliminatory orifices and you have
nine. Unclean things pour from them constantly. That's
while you are alive. But everyone takes special care of
their bodies. They find them good food to eat, nice
clothes to wear, and a comfortable place to live in, so
that they can enjoy themselves and "feel" good. However,
the more comfortable your body is, the more uncomfortable
your self-nature becomes. Your self nature grows defiled,
unclean. No matter how good you are to your body, no matter how much you indulge your emotions and desires, still,
when it comes time to die, your body is going to take off.
No matter how good you have been to it, it's not going to
hang around; it's going to die. When you die, it's not .

over, by any means. Depending on what you did during your
life, you will move to another "home." If you did good
things, you will move to a good "home." If you committed
offenses and planted unwholesome causes, you will move to
a bad place. Perhaps you will fall in with the animals.
Perhaps you will fall into the hells or among the hungry
ghosts. There's nothing fixed about it. Be they men or
women, no matter how beautiful they may have been when
alive, once people are dead, they stink! After a few days
the body starts swelling. Even skinny ones get fat. Then,
they turn mottled green. The most handsome man rots. The
most handsome woman rots. The body then breaks open and
bleeds. At that time, no matter how beautiful they may
have been, no one would love them. Why not? It's the
same person, but, even if it was your father or your
spouse, you wouldn't pay them any attention at all. Even
in the most dedicated relationships, there's never been
a case of the spouse crawling into the coffin of his or
her dead mate. Children don't care to die along with
their parents either. Just look at Gold and Silver (Vol.
I, 48-50) for an example. No matter how they may love
you, they won't accompany you to the grave.

Soon the corpse is crawling with who knows how many
worms. Yecchh! A worm in every hairpore. Eighty-four
thousand hairpores with eighty-four thousand worms. Hah!
The worms crawl in; the worms crawl out! They crawl a-
cross your face and down to your feet and back up to your

head again, looking for those good things to eat, blood and meat. Then the birds join in the feast, should the corpse be out in the open. The p'eng, when short of dragons, will eat human corpses. Once the birds are through with them, there's nothing left but a pile of bleached bones. No one wants the Loved One then, for sure. When the bones are burned only ashes remain. So where did your body go? You were so fond of it, now it's gone.

Secondly, one contemplates feelings as suffering. Thirdly, contemplate thoughts as impermanent. Thoughts change constantly; the process never ends. Fourthly, one contemplates all dharmas as without self. This line of text enjoins us to cultivate the Four Applications of Mindfulness. In this way one can sever attachments.

"ALL OF YOU WORK HARD! DO NOT BE LAX." The workers, that is, the cultivators, are told to work hard. "Working hard" refers to the Four Right Efforts: 1) goodness that has not come forth is caused to come forth; 2) goodness that has already come forth is caused to increase; 3) evil which has not come forth is not permitted to come forth; 4) evil which has already come forth is eradicated. One, in every thought, should attentively cultivate these four and not forget them.

The Four Right Efforts correspond to the first of the Four Additional Practices (explained in detail in the Shurangama Sutra), that of heat. It is like the heat giv-

en off by a drill, when drilling to make a fire. In
one's cultivation one applies the Four Right Efforts and
begins to feel heat. Then, one should increase one's vig-
or, and DO NOT BE LAX. If you gain some skill, don't be
satisfied and quit. The harder you work, the more inconceivable your states become. So the text says, "Work
hard! Don't be lax." Work hard and cultivate the Way.
Don't be lax. Don't allow yourself to doze off and take
naps and so on. It is extremely important that you do
not slack off. It is like drilling for the fire. As you
drill, the wood becomes warm. But if you stop for even
a second, it will cool off and not catch fire. You must
increase your vigor.

BY THIS DEVICE HE DRAWS NEAR TO HIS SON. Cultivating the Four Right Efforts, he has already become neigh-
bors with True Suchness. TO WHOM HE LATER SAYS, "HEY!"
Wake up, right now!! Don't be so confused! "MY BOY!" "Boy"
still refers to the Four Right Efforts, cultivated with
vigor. It says, "Boy!" but, basically in cultivation
there are neither men nor women. Men shouldn't dwell on
the fact that they are men, and women shouldn't dwell on
the fact that they are women. Do not think in terms of
male or female. That's true purity. The Four Right Efforts are associated with the yang aspect of cultivating,
that is, with vigor and strength. The Four Bases of Psychic Power are associated with the yin aspects, the recep-

tivity, etc. If one merely cultivates the Four Right Efforts, one won't obtain the truly wonderful advantages
of cultivation. The Four Right Efforts must be comple-
mented by the Four Bases of Psychic Power. The Four Right
Efforts belong to Wisdom and the Four Bases of Psychic
Power belong to Samadhi. Wisdom is "yang." Samadhi is
"yin." Samadhi and wisdom aid one another. Wisdom aids
samadhi, and samadhi aids wisdom. They help one another
and give rise to the wisdom of non-outflows.

YOU SHOULD STAY HERE AND WORK. Stay here and work,
DON'T GO ELSEWHERE. Don't go anywhere else. This phrase
represents the second of the Four Additional Practices,
Summits. When you get to the summit, you shouldn't move.
Stay here and work. You are at the top. Don't run away.
This is the highest peak, so where else can you go?

I WILL INCREASE YOUR WAGES. Don't run away again.
There's no place to run to. If you run, you will fall.
You will fall into the hells. If you reach the stage of
Summits, you should have Patience, the third of the Four
Additional Practices. You may not feel very comfortable
at this stage, but you must bear it patiently. If you
crave comfort, you will fall to a lowly place, either
among the animals, into the hells, or in with the hungry
ghosts. It may be hard to take, but you must bear with
it. The ancients said,

> If the bitter cold strikes not to the bone,

How can the fragrant plum blossom bloom? Without experiencing the bitter cold of winter, the plum would not smell so piercingly sweet. If you want to reach the top, you must have patience. So the text says, "Do not go elsewhere." This means, don't go study with the outside ways. If you run off with them, or run back into the world, or yield to your desires and improper thoughts, you will fall. You should keep proper thoughts and cultivate well. "I will increase your wages." This means, "You will obtain to the stage of no outflows. Originally, you had a body with outflows and nine holes constantly oozing impure substances. If you cultivate the Proper Path, the food of the Proper Path, and the clothing of the Aids of the Proper Path, you can obtain the stage of no-outflows. In other words, you will certainly certify to the fruit and break through the Delusions of Views and the Delusions of Thought. You will obtain the Stage Beyond Study (Fourth Stage Arhatship) and be without outflows." So the text says, "I will increase your wages," and you will be without outflows.

WHATEVER YOU NEED, the food of the Proper Path and the clothing of the Aids to the Path, you shall have. BE IT POTS, UTENSILS, RICE, FLOUR... "Pots and vessels" represent the Four Dhyanas. "Rice" represents the emptiness of beings (people), while "flour" represents the emptiness of dharmas. The wisdom of the emptiness of beings (people) is a coarse wisdom, while the wisdom of the emptiness of dharmas is a subtle wisdom.

Why is it we can't put anything down? Because we haven't seen through to the emptiness of people. Why can't we let go of anything? Because we haven't realized the emptiness of dharmas. Thus, we can't put anything down, and we can't pick anything up. People and dharmas must be realized as empty; it's not good enough just to speak of them as empty.

Long ago, when Shakyamuni Buddha was still in the world, a layperson asked him to come to his home for offerings. All the Bodhisattvas, great Bhikshus, and the Buddha went there, leaving a young novice at the temple to watch the door. While he was watching the door, another layperson came and asked the Sangha to receive offerings at his house. Since there was no one at the temple but the young novice, off they went. The layperson fed him a delicious, rich lunch, and he ate his fill. However, it's not okay just to eat and run. If you receive offerings of food, you must make an offering of the Dharma in return. The layperson gives wealth, and the left-home person gives Dharma. After lunch the Sangha always lectures on the Dharma, but the young novice did not know how to speak the Dharma! He knew how to eat lunch, for sure, but he had no idea how to speak the Dharma. The layperson was unaware of this, and he knelt very respectfully and asked the young novice to teach him the Dharma. According to the Indian custom, the layperson bows and listens to the Dharma in that position. As he was kneeling there, not raising his head, the young novice employed his great spiritual powers. He got up from his seat, snuck out, ran back to the temple, and locked himself in his room. The layperson had been kneeling for some time, waiting for the Dharma, without hearing any words of wisdom. After about half an hour he raised his head and the young novice was nowhere to be seen! People and dharmas both were empty! What do you think happened? He got enlightened on the spot, understanding the principle of the emptiness of both people and Dharmas! He certified to the First Fruit of Arhatship. He ran to the temple to thank the novice whom he found locked in his room. When he knocked on the door, the young novice was terrified to think he had been followed. In his extreme agitation, he also got enlightened and certified to the First Fruit! That's how it was when the Buddha was in the world. The layperson and the novice both certified to the Fruit and understood the emptiness of people and dharmas. Now, however, it is the Dharma Ending Age, and very few people can understand the emptiness of people and dharmas.

"Rice" and "flour" also represent the Proper Path.

SALT represents impermanence. One should cultivate

the contemplation of impermanence. VINEGAR represents the contemplation of suffering. "Salt" and "vinegar" represent the Aids to the Path. Rice and flour represent the food of the Proper Path. Without salt and vinegar, rice and flour are difficult to eat just plain. Likewise, although the Proper Path should be cultivated, it is not easy without the Aids to the Path.

What are the Aids to the Path? The Thirty-Seven Wings of Enlightenment, that is: the Four Applications of Mindfulness, the Four Bases of Psychic Power, the Four Right Efforts, the Five Roots, the Five Powers, the Seven Bodhi Shares and the Eight-fold Path.

The Four Bases of Psychic Power are:

1. Zeal;

2. Vigor;

3. Mindfulness;

4. Thought.

Zeal means that you should be zealous in your cultivation. You should enjoy cultivating. Then you should be vigorous. You should be constantly vigorous in the six periods of the day and night. With vigor you will then be mindful. The last is "thought," which just refers to Dhyana. You think about your topic, "Who is mindful of the Buddha?" or "Before my parents gave birth to me, what was my original face?" By means of the contemplation of the Four Bases of Psychic Power, one can give rise to various types of samadhis.

The Four Bases of Psychic Power complement the Four Right Efforts. The Four Right Efforts alone will not enable one to gain the state of non-outflows. The combined cultivation of the Four Right Efforts and the Four Bases of Psychic Power and the Four Applications of Mindfulness bring forth the wisdom of non-outflows. So the text says, "Salt or vinegar or other such things," and this includes the other Dharmas such as the Five Roots, the Five Powers, and so on.

DON'T TROUBLE YOURSELF ABOUT IT. You should not doubt yourself. You should deeply believe in these dharmas and have no doubts.

I ALSO HAVE AN OLD, WORN-OUT SERVANT. This represents spiritual powers which can act as extra hands and arms for one. It's an inconceivable state. They can save you a lot of work. Why does it say, "old and worn out?" Because these spiritual powers are extremely weak, soft, as if old, and falling apart. WHOM YOU CAN HAVE IF YOU NEED HIM. If you need the spiritual powers, you can have them. All you have to do is cultivate the Four Bases of Psychic Power. SO PUT YOUR MIND AT REST. This refers to the Third of the Four Additional Practices, that of Patience. At this stage one must stand securely in Patience, rest securely in Patience. One must not indulge in false thinking.

I AM LIKE YOUR FATHER. The Buddha says that he is
like our father. At this point the Elder has not said
right out, "I am your father." He has merely indicated
that he is like a father. The poor son, that is, those
of the Two Vehicles, do not know that they really are
"sons" of the Buddha and that in the future they will become Buddhas.

SO HAVE NO MORE WORRIES. WHY? Don't worry, and don't
go somewhere else, because I AM VERY OLD. The Buddha has
reached the end of the Path and has perfected both the virtue of wisdom and the virtue of cutting off. AND YOU ARE
YOUNG AND STRONG. "You" refers to those of the Two Vehicles. They dwell at the beginning of the Way. They have
not perfected either the virtue of wisdom or the virtue
of cutting off. They lack these two virtues entirely,
as a matter of fact. They are, therefore, said to be
young.

WHENEVER YOU ARE WORKING, YOU ARE NEVER DECEITFUL,
REMISS, ANGRY, HATEFUL, OR GRUMBLING. "Whenever you work"
refers to the Five Roots: faith, vigor, mindfulness, concentration, and wisdom. Because he has the root of faith,
he is not deceitful. Because he has the root of vigor,
he is not remiss or lazy. Because he has the root of
mindfulness, he is free from anger, and because he has
the root of concentration, he has no hatred. Because he
has the root of wisdom, he speaks no words of resentment.

I HAVE NEVER SEEN YOU COMMIT SUCH EVILS AS I HAVE
THE OTHER WORKERS. Since he has the Five Roots, he gives
rise to the Five Powers. He does not commit such evils.
Cultivating the Four Applications of Mindfulness, the
Four Right Efforts, the Four Bases of Psychic Power, the
Five Roots, the Five Powers, all these Dharma-doors,
keeps you free from deceit, laziness, hatred, anger, and
grumbling--evils others often commit.

The "other workers" are those of outside ways. They
cultivate unbeneficial bitter practices.

FROM NOW ON, from today forward, YOU SHALL BE LIKE
MY OWN SON. JUST THEN THE ELDER GAVE HIM A NAME, CALLING
HIM HIS SON. This refers to the Fourth of the Four Addi-
tional Practices, that of Supreme Mundane Dharmas.

THE POOR SON, ALTHOUGH DELIGHTED AT THIS HAPPENING,
STILL REFERRED TO HIMSELF AS A LOWLY WORKER FROM OUTSIDE.
He referred to him self as an outsider. Although he had
met up with the Great Vehicle Buddhadharma, he still
thought of himself as belonging to the Small Vehicle. He
didn't think he was really of the disposition of the Great
Vehicle; he didn't think he was really the Elder's son.

FOR THIS REASON, FOR TWENTY YEARS HE WAS CONSTANTLY
KEPT AT WORK SWEEPING AWAY DUNG. For twenty years, he
worked at sweeping out the dung of the delusions of views
and thought. Twenty years can also represent the principle of unobstruction and the principle of liberation.

Sutra: T. 17a 27
After this, they trusted one another, and he came and went without difficulty. However, he still stayed in the same place as before.

Outline:

> > M4. Bequeathing the inheri-
> > tance.
> >
> > > N1. The inheritance.
> > >
> > > > O1. The son's fa-
> > > > miliarity and
> > > > trustworthiness.

Commentary:

AFTER THIS, means after he had been clearing away dung for some time, getting rid of the delusions of views and thought completely, THEY TRUSTED ONE ANOTHER, AND HE CAME AND WENT WITHOUT DIFFICULTY. Those of the Two Vehicles had gained some attainment in their cultivation of the Way, and they believed in the Great Vehicle Dharma. After this, they didn't feel that it was all that difficult to cultivate the Great Vehicle Dharma. HOWEVER, HE STILL STAYED IN THE SAME PLACE AS BEFORE. Although the Two Vehicles knew that they had a share in Great Vehicle Buddhadharma, still they remained in the Small Vehicle and were unable to give up the Small Vehicle teaching. Thus, they remained at the level of the Small Vehicle, finding it difficult to change their thinking. People's

habits are hard to change. The Buddha taught living beings, hoping that they would turn away from the Small and
go towards the Great, that is, to cultivate the Great Vehicle Dharma, but living beings don't want to change.
When The Lotus Sutra was lectured, at the very beginning
there were five thousand who retreated, that is, got up
and left the assembly. It's definitely not easy to hear
the Buddhadharma or to cultivate it. The Buddha most com-
passionately taught living beings, hoping that they would
all become Buddhas, but living beings just want to slide
down. The Buddha tries to raise them up, teach, and save
them, but they always want to retreat, saying that they
can't become Buddhas. They "stay in the same place,"
they remain in the Two Vehicles.

Sutra: T. 17 a 29
World Honored One: At that time, the
elder grew sick and knew he would die
before long. He said to the poor son, " I
now possess much gold, silver, and jewels,
and my granaries and storehouses are
filled to overflowing. You should know
in detail their quantities and the amounts
to be received and given. Such are my
thoughts, and you should understand
what I mean. What is the reason? You
and I are now no different. You should be
even more careful that nothing be lost."

Outline:

Commentary:

WORLD HONORED ONE, AT THAT TIME, THE ELDER GREW SICK
AND KNEW THAT HE WOULD DIE BEFORE LONG. The Buddha knew
that he was about finished teaching and transforming liv-
ing beings; he was about to enter into Nirvana. HE SAID
TO THE POOR SON, "I NOW POSSESS MUCH GOLD, SILVER, AND
JEWELS. I have many Dharma jewels--the Dhyanas and the
liberations and so on. They are limitless. AND MY GRAN-
ARIES AND STOREHOUSES ARE FILLED TO OVERFLOWING. YOU
SHOULD KNOW IN DETAIL THEIR QUANTITIES AND THE AMOUNTS TO
BE RECEIVED AND GIVEN. SUCH ARE MY THOUGHTS, AND YOU
SHOULD UNDERSTAND WHAT I MEAN. I have already transmitted
my Dharmas to you; you should cultivate accordingly. You
should know the Great Vehicle Buddhadharma. Such are my
thoughts that I turn over all my Great Vehicle Dharma
treasures to you. And you really ought to figure out what
I mean. WHAT IS THE REASON? The Buddha says, "Why is
this?" YOU AND I ARE NOW NO DIFFERENT. YOU SHOULD BE
EVEN MORE CAREFUL THAT NOTHING BE LOST. You are all disciples of the Buddha. We are not different. You are just
like my own son. YOU SHOULD BE EVEN MORE CAREFUL. Pay
close attention THAT NOTHING BE LOST. Don't let the Dhar-

ma be cut off. In every thought propagate the Buddhadharma, and do not allow it to become -extinct.

Sutra: T. 17b4

At that time, the poor son, having received these instructions, took charge of all
the goods, the gold, silver, and precious
gems, as well as the granaries and storehouses, and yet he did not long for so
much as a single meal. He continued to
stay in the same place, still unable to let
go of his lowly thoughts.

Outline:

> P2. Son receives
>
> the command.

Commentary:

AT THAT TIME, after he had been commanded not to lose
anything, that is, not to lose the Great Vehicle doctrine
or the Bodhisattva Path, THE POOR SON, those of the Two Vehicles, HAVING RECEIVED THESE INSTRUCTIONS, the Great Vehicle Buddhadharma, the Buddha's command, TOOK CHARGE OF
ALL THE GOODS, THE GOLD, SILVER, AND PRECIOUS GEMS, AS WELL
AS THE GRANARIES AND STOREHOUSES... The gold represents the
doctrine of the middle way. Silver represents the Real
Truth. The precious gems represent the Buddha's merit,
virtue, and wisdom. The granaries and storehouses represent the Dhyanas, the liberations, and the samadhis. AND

YET HE DID NOT LONG FOR SO MUCH AS A SINGLE MEAL. He was
not like he had been before. He wasn't just concerned with
attaining the low wages of a dung-shoveler. He wasn't living from hand to mouth; he was no longer content with a
small portion. He had started "thinking big." He wasn't
cultivating just for the Small Vehicle; he was now cultivating the Great Vehicle Dharma. HE CONTINUED TO STAY, he
lived IN THE SAME PLACE, in the state of the Two Vehicles.
He still thought that he wasn't cut out to be a Great
Vehicle Bodhisattva. In the Vaipulya Teaching, the
Buddha had told them the of the one-sidedness and scolded
the Small Vehicle and told them the good points of the Great
Vehicle, praising the Perfect Teaching. The Buddha had said
that those of the Small Vehicle who had certified to the
one-sided doctrine were wrong. He scolded those of the Small
Vehicle, calling them withered sprouts and sterile seeds.
He praised the Great Vehicle and commended the Perfect Teaching, saying that the Perfect Teaching was the most wonderful
of the Great Vehicle Dharma-doors. Although those of the Two
Vehicles previously had heard the Buddha speak of the various Dharma-doors, praising the Great Vehicle, they still
felt that they belonged to the Small Vehicle, and so the
text says, "He continued to stay in the same place."

STILL UNABLE TO LET GO OF HIS LOWLY THOUGHTS. "Lowly
thoughts" means being content with small attainment, the
attainment of nirvana with residue. They couldn't put

down their Small Vehicle thoughts to seek diligently the Great Vehicle. They had not yet brought forth their hearts to do so.

Sutra: T. 17b7

After a short while, the father knew that his son had grown more relaxed, that he had accomplished the great resolve and despised his former state of mind. Knowing that his own end was near, he ordered his son to gather together all the relatives, kings, great ministers, kshatriyas, and laypeople. When they had all assembled, he spoke to them saying, "All of you gentlemen should know that this is my son, begotten by me. In a certain city, he left me and ran away to suffer desolation, poverty, and hardship for over fifty years. His original name was such and such, and my name was such. Long ago, in my native city, I anxiously sought him. Suddenly, here, I have found him again! This is really my son. I am really his father. All of my wealth now belongs to my son, and all that has been paid out and taken in is known by him."

Outline:

N2. Passing on the inheritance.

01. Passing on
the inheritance
proper.

Commentary:

AFTER A SHORT WHILE refers to the period of teaching
directly following the Prajna Teaching. During the Prajna
Period, the Buddha was preparing to turn the Teaching to-
ward the Great Vehicle and to pass on his wealth, his inheritance, to his disciples. He hadn't actually done so.
It was not until the Dharma Flower Assembly that he passed
his wealth on.

THE FATHER KNEW THAT HIS SON HAD GROWN MORE RELAXED.
He was no longer afraid. When he first heard the Buddha
speak the Great Vehicle Dharma, he thought the Buddha was
a demon! Now, after some time, his mind understood the
principles of cultivating the Great Vehicle Buddhadharma,
THAT HE HAD ACCOMPLISHED THE GREAT RESOLVE. He had a mind
to cultivate the Great Vehicle Buddhadharma and seek the
Buddha Way. AND DESPISED HIS FORMER STATE OF MIND. He
knew that his former Small Vehicle state was not of much
value, too pitiful. Now, three times he requested the
Great Vehicle Buddhadharma.

KNOWING THAT HIS OWN END WAS NEAR... The Buddha was
about to enter Nirvana, because he had saved the living
beings he was supposed to save and had transformed those
with whom he had affinities. Since there was no one left

to be saved, he was going to enter Nirvana. HE ORDERED
HIS SON, those of the Two Vehicles, TO GATHER TOGETHER ALL
THE RELATIVES, KINGS, GREAT MINISTERS, KSHATRIYAS, AND
LAYPEOPLE... "Relatives" refers to the Bodhisattvas from
other directions who came to the Dharma Assembly to act
as an influential assembly. "Kings" refers to the Twelve
Divisions of the Canon, that is, to all the Sutras the
Buddha spoke. Each Sutra, you might say, is like a coun-
try, and each country has its king. Now, The Dharma Flow-
er Sutra Assembly penetrates the principles of all the
Sutras, and so the "kings" are all gathered together.

The "ministers" are the Equal Enlightenment Bodhisattvas. The "kshatriyas" are the Bodhisattvas on the Ten
Grounds. The Bodhisattvas of the thirty minds are the
"laypeople."

WHEN THEY HAD ALL ASSEMBLED, HE SPOKE TO THEM, SAY-
ING, "ALL OF YOU GENTLEMEN SHOULD KNOW THAT THIS IS MY SON,
BEGOTTEN BY ME." When they had all gathered, the Buddha
said to the Bodhisattvas, "These people of the Two Vehicles are also my own begotten sons. I started teaching
them the Buddhadharma long ago during the time of the Buddha Great Penetration and Supreme Wisdom. Since I caused
them to understand the Buddhadharma, it is as if I gave
birth to them myself. IN A CERTAIN CITY, HE LEFT ME AND
RAN AWAY. They rejected the Great Vehicle Buddhadharma
and ran off to study the Small Vehicle Buddhadharma.   TO

SUFFER DESOLATION, POVERTY, AND HARDSHIP FOR OVER FIFTY
YEARS. He didn't have any belongings. He was very much
alone. "Fifty years" represents the Five Paths of rebirth and also the over fifty positions one passes through
on the way to Buddhahood. HIS ORIGINAL NAME WAS SUCH AND
SUCH, AND MY NAME WAS SUCH AND SUCH. LONG AGO, IN MY NA-
TIVE CITY, I ANXIOUSLY SOUGHT HIM. Those of the Two Vehicles ran off, choosing not to study the Great Vehicle.
This caused the Buddha to worry. Since they refused to
believe, he had to search for some other expedient device.
SUDDENLY, HERE, I HAVE FOUND HIM AGAIN! The Buddha meets
up with those of the Two Vehicles once again and prepares
to set up a clever expedient to teach and transform them.

THIS IS REALLY MY SON. Those of the Two Vehicles
are really the Buddha's sons. It's not like it was before
in the Agama Period, or the Vaipulya Period, or the Prajna Period where it was never said that they were the Buddha's sons. I AM REALLY HIS FATHER. The Buddha is for
sure the father of those of the Two Vehicles. ALL OF MY
WEALTH, all of the Buddha's wealth of Dharma, the wealth
of his merit and virtue and wisdom, NOW BELONGS TO MY SON.
It all belongs to those of the Two Vehicles, and in the
future they shall become Buddhas. AND ALL THAT HAS BEEN
PAID OUT AND TAKEN IN IS KNOWN BY HIM." The Dharma I
taught, from the Avatamsaka Period, through the Agama,
Vaipulya, and Prajna Periods, right up to the Lotus-

Nirvana Period--all my Dharma--my sons of the Two Vehicles know it all. They understand it completely now.

Sutra: T. 17b 15
World Honored One, when the poor son heard what his father had said, he rejoiced greatly, having obtained what he had never had, and he thought, "Originally, I had no thought to seek anything, and now this treasury has come to me of itself."

Outline:

02. Rejoicing at gaining the inheritance.

Commentary:

WORLD HONORED ONE, WHEN THE POOR SON HEARD WHAT HIS FATHER HAD SAID... The Four Great Disciples, including Mahakashyapa spoke to the Buddha saying, "When those of the Two Vehicles heard the Buddha bestow a prediction upon them of their future Buddhahood. HE REJOICED GREATLY, HAVING OBTAINED WHAT HE HAD NEVER HAD. They had never been so happy. They congratulated themselves on their good fortune.

"ORIGINALLY, I HAD NO THOUGHT TO SEEK ANYTHING. Originally, I hadn't hoped to become a Great Vehicle Bodhisattva or to be a real son of the Buddha. It never occurred to me. AND NOW, THIS TREASURY HAS COME TO ME OF ITSELF. All of the Buddha's wisdom, merit, and virtue,

Dharma wealth and treasure, has come to me. I didn't expend the slightest bit of effort to attain it. I'm really
lucky!"

Sutra: T.17 b 18
World Honored One, the great and wealthy elder is the Thus Come One. We are all like the Buddha's sons.

Outline:

> K1. Correlation of
> analogy with Dharma.
> L1. Correlating
> separation of
> father and son.

Commentary:

WORLD HONORED ONE, THE GREAT AND WEALTHY ELDER, whom
in this analogy we have just presented, IS THE THUS COME
ONE, the Buddha. WE ARE ALL LIKE THE BUDDHA'S SONS. All
of us Sound Hearers now know that we are the Buddha's sons.
Originally, one could just say, "We _are_ the Buddha's sons.
But the text says, "We are all _like_ the Buddha's sons."
They aren't his sons in the truest sense of the word. The
Bodhisattvas are the Buddha's real, true sons. Sound Hearers are _like_ the Buddha's sons. The Sound Hearers don't
yet realize that they are, in fact, walking the Bodhisat-
tva Path, and so they say they are like the Buddha's sons.

Sutra: T. 17 b 18
The Thus come One always says that we are his sons.

Outline:

> L2. Correlation of
>
> father and son
>
> meeting again.

Commentary:

THE THUS COME ONE, the World Honored One, in the Avatamsaka, Agama, Vaipulya, and Prajna Periods continually said, "All living beings are the Buddha's sons."

Sutra: T. 17 b 19
World Honored One, because of the three kinds of suffering, we have suffered much torment in the midst of births and deaths. Deluded and ignorant, we clung to petty dharmas.

Outline:

> L3. Correlation of
>
> bringing the son
>
> back.
>
>> M1. Correlation
>>
>> of sending peo-
>>
>> ple after him.

Commentary:

WORLD HONORED ONE, BECAUSE OF THE THREE KINDS OF SUFFERING, that is, 1) the suffering within suffering, which refers to all the misery we must undergo as a result of having a physical body. As the body gradually decays one undergoes, 2) the suffering of decay. As this process continues, thought after thought, without interruption, one undergoes, 3) the suffering of process. Because of these three sufferings, IN THE MIDST OF BIRTHS AND DEATHS, life after life, death after death, WE HAVE SUFFERED MUCH TORMENT. In the burning house of the Triple World, we are burned by the blaze of the Five Skandhas.

DELUDED AND IGNORANT, WE CLUNG TO PETTY DHARMAS. We have taken a thief as our own son, turned our backs on enlightenment to join with the defilement of the mundane world. We are stupid and lacking wisdom, because we are deeply deluded by our ignorance and our afflictions. Not only that, we preferred the lesser dharmas, the Small Vehicle, failing to understand the Great Vehicle Buddhadharma.

Sutra: T. 17b21

Today, the World Honored One has caused us to think about getting rid of the dung of frivolous discussions of the Dharma. We increased our vigor to earn one day's wage of Nirvana. Having attained this, our hearts rejoiced greatly, and we were content, saying to ourselves that, through our diligence and vigor, what we had gained in the Buddhadharma was plentiful.

Outline:

> M2. Correlating
>
> sending two peo-
>
> ple after him.
>
> > N1. Correla-
> >
> > ting the in-
> >
> > structions.

Commentary:

TODAY, THE WORLD HONORED ONE, now in the Dharma Flower Assembly, HAS CAUSED US TO THINK ABOUT GETTING RID OF THE DUNG OF FRIVOLOUS DISCUSSIONS OF THE DHARMA. The petty, small vehicle dharmas we studied before are but frivolous assertions about the Dharma. This refers to the afflictions involved with views and thought. WE INCREASED OUR VIGOR. We Sound Hearers increased our vigor, cultivating the small vehicle, fearing birth and death and suffering and impermanence. We worked real hard at our cultivation. TO EARN ONE DAY'S WAGE OF NIRVANA. We gained one-sided nirvana with residue. HAVING ATTAINED THIS, OUR HEARTS REJOICED GREATLY, AND WE WERE CONTENT, SAYING TO OURSELVES THAT THROUGH OUR DILIGENCE AND VIGOR, WHAT WE HAVE GAINED IN THE BUDDHADHARMA IS PLENTIFUL. Attaining this one-sided nirvana, we are very happy and content with this little portion, something we have never had before. That's it; we've made it!

So we see that in cultivating Dhyana, if one obtains some small state, one should not be satisfied. On should increase one's vigor and make further progress. They said, "THROUGH OUR DILIGENCE AND VIGOR, working industriously as we have, WHAT WE HAVE GAINED IN THE BUDDHADHARMA IS PLENTIFUL. We've got just too much!" Really, they had obtained one small speck of the Buddhadharma, not a lot.

Sutra: T.17b24
However, the World Honored One, knowing all along that our minds were attached to lowly desires and took delight in petty dharmas, let us go our own way and did not specify to us saying, "You are all to have a share in the treasury of the Thus Come One's knowledge and vision."

Outline:

N2. Correlating the intention.

Commentary:

HOWEVER, THE WORLD HONORED ONE, even though we ran,
the Buddha KNOWING ALL ALONG THAT OUR MINDS... He knew it
all the time, knew that our minds WERE ATTACHED TO LOWLY
DESIRES, base cravings: 1) wealth, 2) sex, 3) fame, 4)
food, and 5) sleep. AND TOOK DELIGHT IN PETTY DHARMAS.
They were attached to the Small Vehicle Dharma. LET US
GO OUR WAY. And so the Buddha just let them go; he did
not speak of the Great Vehicle. AND DID NOT SPECIFY TO
US, SAYING how with the Great Vehicle one can become a
Buddha, practice the Bodhisattva Way, teach and transform
living beings, and purify the Buddhalands. He didn't
speak of the state of the Great Vehicle.

"YOU ARE ALL TO HAVE A SHARE IN THE TREASURY OF THE
THUS COME ONE's KNOWLEDGE AND VISION." In the future,
you will have the Thus Come One's wisdom, his knowledge,
and vision, and the treasuries of the Buddha. He knew
that they liked the Small Vehicle, and so formerly he never told them that they were the genuine sons of the Buddha.

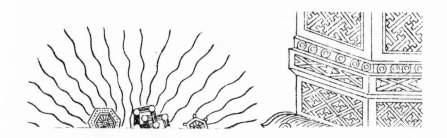

Sutra: T17b26

The World Honored One, using the power of expedient devices, has spoken of the Thus Come One's wisdom. Having gained from the Buddha the one day's wage of Nirvana, we took it to be a great attainment; we had no ambition to seek the Great Vehicle. Besides, the wisdom of the Thus Come One had been set forth for the sake of the Bodhisattvas, and so he held no expectations regarding it. What is the reason? The Buddha knew that our minds took delight in petty dharmas. He used the power of expedients to teach us in the appropriate manner, and we did not know that we were truly the Buddha's sons.

Outline:

> > L4. Correlating the
> >
> > inheritance.
> >
> > > M1. Correlating
> > >
> > > the inheritance
> > >
> > > itself.

Commentary:

The World Honored One did not tell the Small Vehicle people of the Great Vehicle directly. He used expedients to teach them of the Buddha's wisdom. "THE WORLD HONORED ONE, USING THE POWER OF EXPEDIENT DEVICES, HAS SPOKEN OF THE THUS COME ONE'S WISDOM. All of us Sound Hearers who studied the Dharma under the Buddha, HAVING GAINED FROM

THE BUDDHA THE ONE DAY'S WAGE OF NIRVANA, attaining the
one-sided nirvana with residue, like laborers who get paid
by the day, TOOK IT TO BE A GREAT ATTAINMENT, a big thing.
WE HAD NO AMBITION TO SEAK THE GREAT VEHICLE. We had no
inclination to seek the wonderful doctrine of the Great
Vehicle.

   "BESIDES, THE WISDOM OF THE THUS COME ONE HAD BEEN SET
FORTH FOR THE SAKE OF THE BODHISATTVAS, AND SO WE HELD NO
EXPECTATIONS REGARDING IT." The Buddha had assisted Shariputra and Subhuti in the teaching of Prajna. Shariputra
and Subhuti thought it wasn't their own power. They
thought it was the Buddha's power that enabled them to
speak Prajna, and so they had neither hope for the Great
Vehicle nor ambition to practice the Bodhisattva Path themselves. "WHAT IS THE REASON? THE BUDDHA KNEW THAT OUR
MINDS TOOK DELIGHT IN PETTY DHARMAS. The Buddha knew that
we of the Small Vehicle were quite attached to our Small
Vehicle. HE USED THE POWER OF EXPEDIENTS TO TEACH US IN
THE APPROPRIATE MANNER. He taught us the Dharma according
to our dispositions. AND WE DID NOT KNOW THAT WE WERE
TRULY THE BUDDHA'S SONS. We of the Two Vehicles didn't
know that, all the time, we were the Buddha's sons; we
didn't understand the doctrine of the Great Vehicle. We,
too, are the Buddha's sons!"

Sutra: T. 17 c 3

Now we know that the World Honored One is by no means ungenerous with the Buddha's wisdom. Why? From of old, we truly have been the Buddha's sons, and yet we delighted only in petty dharmas. If we had thought to delight in the great, the Buddha would then have spoken for us the Great Vehicle Dharma. This Sutra speaks of only One Vehicle. In the past, in the presence of the Bodhisattvas, the Buddha had belittled the Sound Hearers who delight in lesser dharmas, but he was actually employing the Great Vehicle in teaching and transforming them.

Outline:

M2. Correlating

the bequest.

N1. Passing it

on.

Commentary:

"We didn't know before that those of the Small Vehicle were also the Buddha's sons, but NOW WE KNOW, here in the Dharma Flower Assembly, THAT THE WORLD HONORED ONE IS BY NO MEANS UNGENEROUS WITH THE BUDDHA'S WISDOM. It was not that the Buddha didn't want to teach those of the Two Vehicles. WHY? FROM OF OLD, WE TRULY HAVE BEEN THE BUDDHA'S SONS, and limitless aeons ago we had already been taught and transformed by the Buddha, and the seeds of

the Great Vehicle had been planted in us. We were the
Buddha's real sons all the time, but we were like the poor
son who ran away from home and failed to recognize his
father. But now we know we didn't study the Great Vehicle
Dharma because WE DELIGHTED IN PETTY DHARMAS, in the Small
Vehicle Dharma. IF WE HAD THOUGHT TO DELIGHT IN THE
GREAT, if we had delighted in the Great Vehicle Buddha-
dharma, THE BUDDHA WOULD THEN HAVE SPOKEN FOR US THE GREAT
VEHICLE DHARMA. The Buddha would have placed before them
the entire Great Vehicle's wonderful doctrine. NOW, THIS
SUTRA, The Dharma Flower Sutra, SPEAKS OF ONLY ONE VEHI-
CLE, the Buddha Vehicle. It says there is only the Bud-
dha Vehicle; there is no other vehicle. IN THE PAST, IN
THE PRESENCE OFTHE BODHISATTVAS, in the Vaipulya and Praj-
na Assemblies, THE BUDDHA HAD BELITTLED THE SOUND HEARERS
WHO DELIGHT IN LESSER DHARMAS, he scolded those of the
Small Vehicle and praised the Great Vehicle and the Perfect Teaching. He scolded those of the Two Vehicles, saying 'You Sound Hearers are gutless. You have no future
at all and no light, either. You are like withered sprouts
and sterile seeds. You are stuck to your small dharmas.'
BUT HE WAS ACTUALLY EMPLOYING THE GREAT VEHICLE IN TEACH-
ING AND TRANSFORMING THEM. He was bestowing the Provisional for the sake of the Real. The small vehicle dharmas were set forth for the sake of the Real. Now, in the
Dharma Flower Assembly, the Provisional Teaching of the

Small Vehicle is dispensed with, and the real Dharma is re-
vealed, the real, wondrous doctrine."

Sutra: T.17 c 8

Therefore, we say that originally we had not hoped for or sought anything, and yet now these great jewels of the Dharma King have come to us of themselves. That which the Buddha's sons should attain, we have already attained.

Outline:

> N2. Correlat-
>
> ing the Re-
>
> joicing.

Commentary:

"THEREFORE, WE SAY THAT ORIGINALLY WE HAD NOT HOPED FOR
OR SOUGHT ANYTHING. We figured we were just Small Vehicle
types. We didn't dare raise our hopes too high. AND YET,
NOW THIS GREAT JEWEL OF THE DHARMA KING HAS COME TO US OF
ITSELF. After observing the potentials of living beings,
the Buddha speaks the Dharma which accords with their dispositions. Some have mature dispositions, and others are
still immature. Now, in the Dharma Flower Assembly the
Dharma King's Great Jewels, all the Buddha's Dharmas, have
spontaneously arrived. The Buddha has opened the Provisional to reveal the Real. Previously, for the sake of the
One Buddha Vehicle, he taught the Three Vehicles--those of

the Bodhisattvas, Conditioned Enlightened Ones, and the Sound Hearers. Here, in the Dharma Flower Assembly, he returns the three back to the one. The Three Vehicles revert to the One Buddha Vehicle. They didn't expend the slightest bit of effort to gain the Buddha's inheritance, that is, to gain the entire Dharma treasury of the Buddha.

"THAT WHICH THE BUDDHA'S SONS SHOULD ATTAIN, the wealth, the Dharma jewels of the Buddha, WE HAVE ALREADY ATTAINED. We have got them all."

Sutra: T. 17c10
At that time, Mahakashyapa, wishing to restate this meaning, spoke verses, saying,
We, on this day,
Hearing the sound of the Buddha's teaching,
Jump for joy! –
Gaining what we never had.
The Buddha says that Sound Hearers,
Shall become Buddhas in the future.
A cluster of supreme gems,
We have gained, without our seeking.

Outline:

I2. Verses.

J1. Verses of Dharma.

Commentary:

AT THAT TIME, MAHAKASHYAPA, representing the four
great disciples: Mahakashyapa, Mahamaudgalyayana, Mahakatyayana, and Subhuti, wanted to speak the doctrine yet
again, WISHING TO RESTATE THIS MEANING, SPOKE VERSES SAY-
ING...

Tomorrow, the second six-week summer session begins.
It must be entirely different from the first six weeks.
The first six weeks was "a snap," and no one really cultivated. Originally, although there weren't a lot of
people, if they hadn't been so lax, there might have been
several who became enlightened. But, as soon as they got
lax, they were off by a hair's breadth from gaining the
response needed to get enlightened. One disciple's
skill at meditation is very good. He has broken through
the Three Gates, but he hasn't opened his Five Eyes. If
he hadn't been so lazy during the first six weeks, they
would have opened right away. But, since he was afraid
of hard work and like to take it easy, they still haven't
really opened. They have sort of opened--a small state.
If you want to make progress in your work, you have to
toil bitterly, unafraid of suffering and difficulty. You
have to work straightforwardly to have success. Those
who attend the second session must bear up under the
struggle and toil. Don't forget that you came to the
session to gain advantage, to gain some genuine wisdom
and real understanding of the Buddhadharma and to under-

stand the basic principles of being human. If you want
to do that, then don't be afraid of suffering or hardship,
and don't sneak off to take it easy! At all times, work
hard. When it's time to meditate, meditate. When it's
time to investigate Buddhism, do that. During the lectures, pay attention. Everyone should write notes and
don't miss a day. Don't be lazy for a single day or a
single moment. Then, in these six weeks you won't have
wasted your time. If you just fiddle around and don't
really work, it will be a pitiful waste. You could have
been out taking a vacation or seeing the sights and having a good time. If you aren't going to cultivate, why
come to the Buddhist Lecture Hall? You could be having
a good time somewhere else instead of wasting your time.
We don't waste time here. We really work hard.

The following section of verse is intended to re-
peat the principles set forth in the preceding prose section in a simplified manner. You could also say it is to
present the principles in a more detailed manner. You
could say that the prose was detailed, and the verse was
simplified; you could also say that the prose was simplified and the verse gives more detail, whichever you like.
In any case, Mahakashyapa was responding to the needs of
living beings when he spoke the verses.

WE, Sound Hearers, ON THIS DAY/ HEARING THE SOUND

OF THE BUDDHA'S TEACHING/ the doctrines he has set forth to to teach and transform living beings, JUMP FOR JOY! We are so happy. We jump because we are just too happy. Super happy! Why? Because we never had such Dharma jewels before, and now we have attained them, GAINING WHAT WE NEVER HAD. We have attained Dharma which we never had before."

What is this rare Dharma? The Buddha had not bestowed predictions upon Sound Hearers before. Now, the Buddha says that Sound Hearers have the chance to become Buddhas. "THE BUDDHA SAYS THAT SOUND HEARERS/ SHALL BECOME BUDDHAS IN THE FUTURE/ Hearing that we shall become Buddhas, we feel as if A CLUSTER OF SUPREME GEMS/ WE HAVE GAINED, WITHOUT OUR SEEKING. We didn't seek for these unsurpassed Dharma treasures; they came to us of their own accord.

Sutra: T. 17 C 13
> It is like a youth,
> Who, young and ignorant,
> Ran away from his father
> To another distant land,
> Roaming from country to country
> For fifty years and more.

Outline:

J2. Verses of analogy.

K1. Verses setting up the
analogy.

L1. Verses of father
and son being separa-
ted.

M1. Verses of son
turning his back
on his father and
running off.

Commentary:

IT IS LIKE A YOUTH/ WHO YOUNG AND IGNORANT/ Mahakashyapa now restates the analogy. It is like a small child
who has no real understanding. He RAN AWAY FROM HIS FA-
THER/ He doesn't realize that he should stay close to his
parents. He forsakes his father. He gives him away! Who
does he give him away to? Nobody wants him! At any rate,
he leaves his father and runs away. Why did he run away?
He was just a child and didn't know what he was doing.

TO ANOTHER, DISTANT LAND/ The countries represent the
three realms. ROAMING FROM COUNTRY TO COUNTRY/ He roamed
from one to the next, like water flowing from stream to river to the sea. He went around to all the different countries. He was, as you say, on a "bum trip." FOR FIFTY
YEARS AND MORE. That represents the Five Paths. There are
originally Six Paths, but the path of asuras pervades the
other five, so we just say five paths.

Sutra: T. 17 C 15

> His father, worried about him,
> Sought him in the four directions
> Until, tired of the search,
> He stopped in a certain city,
> Where he built himself a house
> And amused himself with the five
>   desires.
> His household was large and wealthy,
> With much gold and silver,
> Mother-of-pearl, carnelian,
> Real pearls, and lapis lazuli,
> Elephants, horses, cattle, and sheep,
> Hand-drawn carts, palanquins, and
>   chariots,
> Husbandsmen and servants,
> And a multitude of subjects.
> The profits from his trade
> Extended to the other countries.
> Traders and merchants
> Were present everywhere.
> Multitudes in the hundreds of
>   millions
> Surrounded him reverentially.
> And always, by kings,
> He was cherished and remembered.
> The ministers and noble clans
> All honored him.
> For these reasons,
> Those who came and went were many.
> Such was his nobility, wealth,
> And his great authority.

Outline:

M2. Verse of seek-
ing his son and
stopping halfway.

HIS FATHER, WORRIED ABOUT HIM/ His father had hoped
his son would see him through his old age, but he ran
away instead! So he was worried, and grew older and older every day, thinking about him until he got wrinkles
on his face. Now, the Sound Hearers are like children.
They left the Buddha and ran outside. The Buddha wanted
to save the Sound Hearers and looked for them everywhere,
"worried."

SOUGHT HIM IN THE FOUR DIRECTIONS/ UNTIL, TIRED OF
THE SEARCH/ After a while he got tired. HE STOPPED IN A
CERTAIN CITY/ This represents Shakyamuni Buddha looking
for living beings to save and coming to the Saha world.
WHERE HE BUILT HIMSELF A HOUSE/ AND AMUSED HIMSELF WITH
THE FIVE DESIRES/ The five desires: wealth, sex, fame,
food, and sleep. They are the five roots of hell. Does
this mean that the Buddha was greedy for the five desires?
No. It's just an analogy. The Five Desires represent the
living beings in the five paths that the Buddha wants to
save, to lead to Buddhahood. So don't get it wrong and
think, "If the Buddha is attached to the five desires, why
shouldn't I be attached to them?"

HIS HOUSEHOLD WAS LARGE AND WEALTHY/ The Buddha is the wealthiest person there is. WITH MUCH GOLD AND SIL-VER/ an uncountable amount, MOTHER-OF-PEARL, CARNELIAN/ ELEPHANTS, HORSES, CATTLE, AND SHEEP/ HAND-DRAWN CARTS, like the carts the Emperor's concubines would ride in in ancient times. They were even more comfortable than our cars nowadays, and since they were hand-drawn, they had better suspension systems. In Manchuria, the cars have terrible suspension. They bounce up and down, and your butt gets sore from riding in them! PALANQUINS are the carts that the Emperors ride in. CHARIOTS/ are vehicles in general. This great elder was very wealthy, and so he had the best of everything. HUSBANDSMEN AND SERVANTS-AND A MULTITUDE OF SUBJECTS/

THE PROFITS FROM HIS TRADE/ EXTENDED TO THE OTHER COUNTRIES/ His investments extended into neighboring lands. TRADERS AND MERCHANTS/ The traveling traders and the sedentary merchants WERE PRESENT EVERYWHERE/ MULTITUDES IN THE HUNDREDS OF MILLIONS/ SURROUNDED HIM REVERENTIALLY/ A thousand, ten thousand, million of them AND ALWAYS, BY KINGS/ HE WAS CHERISHED AND REMEMBERED/ The kings of other countries thought of him fondly. MINISTERS AND NOBLE CLANS/ ALL HONORED HIM/ FOR THESE REASONS/ THOSE WHO CAME AND WENT WERE MANY/ SUCH WAS HIS NOBILITY, WEALTH/ AND GREAT AUTHOR-ITY. "Great authority" means that the Buddha is complete with all dharmas, and so he is the King of all Dharmas.

Because he possesses all dharmas, he is reverentially surrounded by all the Great Bodhisattvas, Sound Hearers, and
Arhats. The Buddha occupies the highest position of authority. Also, the Buddhas of the ten directions surround and
protect the Buddha, and the Bodhisattvas of the ten directions protect his Bodhimanda. The Buddha turns the wheel
of the unsurpassed and wonderful Dharma to teach and transform boundless numbers of living beings.

Sutra: T. 17 c 25
> But then, as he grew old and decrepit,
> He was filled with worry for his son.
> Morning and evening, his only thought
> was,
> "My time of death is drawing near.
> My foolish son has left me now,
> For over fifty years.
> The things in my granaries and store-
> houses –
> Whatever shall I do with them?"

Outline:

M3. Verses of his

father's worries.

Commentary:

The Elder may have had great wealth, BUT THEN, AS HE
GREW OLD AND DECREPIT/ his health declined. Why did his
health decline? Because HE WAS FILLED WITH WORRY FOR HIS

SON/ He spent all his energy worrying about his son. So he wasn't so strong and healthy anymore. He was like an old piece of dry wood. In fact, the Chinese word for decrepit, 朽 hsiu, is the wood radical 木 plus the word for decline 丂 . There is a saying, "A rotten piece of wood cannot be carved," as soon as you take a chisel to it, it crumbles. "A wall of mud cannot be painted." If the wall is made of mud, you cannot paint frescoes on it; no matter how pretty the flowers or the scenery, it won't look good on a plain mud wall. This means that when people get older, they grow more compassionate, and they think about their children a lot. The Elder thought about his son. MORNING AND EVENING HIS ONLY THOUGHT WAS/ "Where is he? He ran away when he was very small. I haven't been able to find him anywhere." When a child runs away from home, it's hard for the parents to locate him again. But, if the child wants to return to his parents, it's very easy; all he has to do is go back home. So, the Elder was "filled" with worry for his son. He thought of him every single day. "Morning" and "evening," he thought of him. He couldn't sleep at night wondering where he had gone. He had terrible insomnia. They didn't have sleeping pills in those days, so he just laid there and stared at the ceiling all night. "MY TIME OF DEATH IS DRAWING NEAR"/ I'm not getting any younger. I don't know which day I will die.

This reminds me of a story. Long ago, there were three old people who got together to drink some wine--or perhaps some tea. It's not fixed. If I say wine, then those of you who like wine will find your mouths watering. So, let's not say for sure what they were drinking--maybe tea or coffee. Or maybe they were just eating some vegetables. Anyway, one of them was sixty, one was seventy, and one was eighty. The one who was sixty always liked to get his two cents in, and so he said, "Old brothers, we are eating vegetables here together this year. But next year, who knows which one of us won't be here?" What he meant, of course, was that they didn't know which one of them would be dead. They were all pretty old. The seventy-year old man thought, "That's sensible enough, but I bet I can think of something better." Then he said, "Hey Old Buddy! That remark was really off the wall you know, tonight when we take off our shoes and socks and go to sleep, we don't know who will be around to put them back on in the morning!" Well, the sixty-year old didn't have a thing to say in reply to that.

It so happened that the eighty-year-old was especially fond of the sixty-year old, and when he saw that the seventy-year old had put him down, he retorted, "Hey! You think you topped him with your statement, there. Try this one, "When I take in one breath, I don't know if I'll be around to exhale it!"

We can see that the eighty-year old was the clearest
about the question of birth and death, and so he out-talked
them both. The other two were most impressed and thought,
"He's right. We don't know if we'll get our next breath.
There's nothing left for us to do but cultivate like crazy
and meditate and recite the Buddha's name and go to Sutra
lectures."

You may wonder, "If they do those things, will they
not die?"

Not necessarily.

"Then what use are they?"

Although it won't prevent them from dying, they will
make a difference in _how_ they die. Before, they drew in a
breath and didn't know if they were going to be around to
exhale it. But, if one works hard at cultivating the Way,
meditates, recites Sutras and the Buddha's name, then if
one wants to exhale, one can exhale. If you don't want
to inhale again, you can do that, too. You have control
over it. If you think, "I want to stay around for a few
more meals," then you can. If you think, "I've had it.
No more meals for me. It's all pretty meaningless. This
stinking skin-bag is just too much work. I have to take
it to the toilet everyday at the very least. And then
when I move the food out, I have to put more food in.
It's too much trouble. I don't want it anymore. I'm going to put it down." then you can just let it go.

MY FOOLISH SON HAS LEFT ME NOW/ My child has not returned. He's really just too stupid. Stupid, stupid... never thinks of his father who is so old. FOR OVER FIFTY YEARS/ In the Five Paths he turns. THE THINGS IN MY GRANARIES AND STOREHOUSES/ all the treasures, all the fine things, WHATEVER SHALL I DO WITH THEM? What am I going to do? Huh?" What would you do?

Sutra: T. 17C27
Then the poor son,
Seeking clothing and food,
Went from city to city,
From country to country,
Sometimes getting something,
Sometimes getting nothing.
Starving, emaciated,
Covered with scabs,
He went on his way until eventually,
He arrived in the city where his
    father lived.

Outline:

M4. Verses of son arriving in father's city.

Commentary:

The wealthy elder couldn't sleep at night, thinking of his son. And he didn't have any appetite. Why couldn't he sleep? Because he was too wealthy. He didn't know what to do with it all. So he was very worried. THEN THE POOR SON/ who had run away, that is, those of the Two Vehicles who had run off, SEEKING CLOTHING AND FOOD/ They were seeking the Dharma. WENT FROM CITY TO CITY/ They passed through the twelve places: the eye, ear, nose, tongue, body, mind, plus form, sound, smell, taste, tangible objects, and dharmas. They also passed through the eighteen realms of sense, that is, the six sense organs, plus the six sense objects, plus the six corresponding discriminating consciousnesses. For example, the eye organ sees the object of form, and the eye-consciousness arises. Ears hear sounds, and the ear-consciousness arises. The nose smells odors, and nose-consciousness arises. The tongue tastes flavors, and tongue-consciousness arises. The body feels touch, and body-consciousness arises. The mind cognizes dharmas, and mind-consciousness arises. When there is no state manifesting, then there is no discrimination. But, once a state manifests, then there is discrimination, and the twelve places extend into the eighteen realms. Passing through the twelve places and the eighteen realms, they then sought the food of the Proper Path and the clothing of the Aids to the Path. So the text says, "Went from city to city." They went from the city of eye to the city of ear, and on to the nose, tongue, body, and mind.

FROM COUNTRY TO COUNTRY/ The eye saw forms and went

to eye-consciousness. The ears heard sounds and went to
ear-consciousness. The nose smelled odors and went to
nose-consciousness. The tongue tasted flavors and went
to tongue consciousness. The body felt tangible objects
and went to body-consciousness. The mind cognized dharmas and went to mind-consciousness. Thus, they went from
country to country.

SOMETIMES GETTING SOMETHING/ This refers to those
with the good roots but with outflows, doing good deeds,
but not ultimate good. It means doing superficial things.
SOMETIMES GETTING NOTHING/ refers to non-outflow good
roots. It means doing good without outflows, that is,
ending birth and death and entering nirvana. Although
one ends birth and death and enters nirvana, there is,
in actuality, nothing attained, for birth and death is
just nirvana, and nirvana is just birth and death. There
is nothing attained, and so the text says SOMETIMES GET-
TING NOTHING.

STARVING, EMACIATED/ This doesn't mean that he was
starving because he had nothing to eat. Rather, he was
starving because he had not attined the Great Vehicle
Buddhadharma. Once one has "eaten" the doctrine of the
Great Vehicle, one is full. Those of the Two Vehicles
who have not yet understood the Great Vehicle are hungry,
famished! "Emaciated" means they haven't obtained the
great function, and they haven't obtained great merit and

virtue. COVERED WITH SCABS/ His body was covered with sores and scabs. This means that one is confused about true principle and takes the false to be true; one takes a thief as one's own son, or we can say that one casts away the root and seeks the branches. Not understanding true principle, one gives rise to view delusions and thought delusions.

What are view delusions? View delusions refer to giving rise to greed and love when faced with a state. Why do you give rise to greed and love? Because you view the state and become confused. You see it and don't understand it. So, view delusion arises out of ignorance. Because you have not broken through your basic ignorance, when faced with a state you give rise to greed and love.

View delusion refers to what you see. Thought delusion takes place within the mind and is not related to what you see. You lack understanding, but go ahead and use the sixth (mind) consciousness to discriminate all kinds of things: good, bad, right, wrong, long and short, etc., etc. Most people think the discriminating mind is a good thing. Actually, it is the worst thing! You discriminate and discriminate until you're entirely confused. Once you get confused, you do stupid things. Giving rise to view delusion and thought delusion is what the text means by "covered with scabs." Most people think these delusions are just great. They don't know what they really are.

HE WENT ON HIS WAY UNTIL EVENTUALLY/ Step by step, he went from country to country until HE ARRIVED IN THE CITY WHERE HIS FATHER LIVED, where the Buddha was dwelling. Those of the Two Vehicles ran outside looking for the Dharma everywhere. They sought it everwhere but found no ultimate Dharma and finally wound up back with the Buddha.

Sutra: T. 18 a 2

> Hiring himself out along the way,
> He finally reached his father's house.
> At that time, the elder,
> Within his gateway,
> Was covered by a large canopy,
> And seated on a Lion-throne,
> Surrounded by his retinue,
> And various attendants.
> Some of them were counting up
> His gold, silver, and other valuables.
> His income and expenses were
> Recorded there on ledgers.
> When the poor son saw his father,
> Of such nobility and wealth,
> He said, "This must be a king,
> Or the equal of a king."
> In fright, he reproved himself,
> "Why have I come here?"
> And further to himself, he said,
> "If I stay here long,
> I may be oppressed
> And forced to go to work."
> Having had this thought,
> He hurriedly ran off
> To a poor village, asking
> To be hired out to work.

Outline:

> L2. Verses of father
> and son meeting again.
> M1. Verses of son
> seeing the father.

Commentary:

HIRING HIMSELF OUT ALONG THE WAY/ The poor son hired himself out to do odd jobs to keep himself alive. HE FINALLY REACHED HIS FATHER'S HOUSE/ Without even realizing it himself, he arrived at his father's house. AT THAT TIME, THE ELDER/ The greatly wealthy Elder, the one who had lost his son, WITHIN HIS GATEWAY/ He was within the confines of his property, WAS COVERED BY A LARGE CANOPY/ AND SEATED ON A LION-THRONE/ It was an especially expensive seat. SURROUNDED BY HIS RETINUE/ many members of his household, AND VARIOUS ATTENDANTS/ He had many people to help him. SOME OF THEM WERE COUNTING UP/ HIS GOLD, SILVER, AND OTHER VALUABLES/ HIS INCOME AND EXPENSES WERE/ RECORDED THERE ON LEDGERS/ People were figuring his accounts for him, recording the transactions in detail. The ledger represents the Four Vast Vows:

> I vow to save the boundless number of
> living beings.
> I vow to sever the endless afflictions.
> I vow to study the limitless Dharma-doors.
> I vow to attain the Supreme Buddha Way.

If one makes the Four Vast Vows, one has been "written in the ledger" to become a Buddha. One has a guarantee. The act of writing in the ledger is an analogy for cultivating the Way.

WHEN THE POOR SON SAW HIS FATHER/ OF SUCH NOBILITY AND WEALTH/ HE SAID, "THIS MUST BE A KING/ OR THE EQUAL TO A KING"/ This person is so noble and wealthy, he must certainly be a royal personage of one sort or another. IN FRIGHT, HE REPROVED HIMSELF/ He was scared practically out of his wits, and he blamed himself saying, "What did you come here for? This is a king's place! You don't belong here! Whatever possessed you to come here?" He was hard on himself. "Why, you are just a poor nobody. How did you get in the king's house?" AND FURTHER TO HIMSELF HE SAID/ "IF I STAY HERE LONG/ I MAY BE OPPRESSED/ I better not hang around here gawking! These people have a lot of clout. I'm sure to get pushed around. AND FORCED TO GO TO WORK"/ I'll have to work for them. HAVING HAD THIS THOUGHT/ HE RAN HURRIEDLY RAN OFF/ He ran off as fast as he could, hoping to avoid a scene.

TO A POOR VILLAGE, ASKING/ TO BE HIRED OUT TO WORK/ He didn't dare speak with the rich people. He went to the poor section of town asking for work. He felt more at ease with the poor folks, and he asked them if they had any odd jobs he could do.

Sutra: T. 18a10
> Just then, the elder,
> Seated on the Lion-throne,
> Saw his son at a distance,
> And silently recognized him.

Outline:

M2. Verses of father

seeing son.

Commentary:

JUST THEN, THE ELDER/ The Elder, the Buddha, then
SEATED ON THE LION-THRONE/ so high and grand, SAW HIS SON
AT A DISTANCE/ The minute he saw him, he knew that it was
his own son, the son who had run off when he was quite
small. AND SILENTLY RECOGNIZED HIM/ He didn't tell anyone.

Sutra: T. 18a12
> He then commanded his attendants
> To seize him and bring him back.
> The poor son cried out in alarm,
> And fainted, falling to the ground.
> "These people have caught me!
> I shall certainly be killed!
> Why, for food and clothing's sake
> Did I come to this place?"
> The elder knew that his son
> Was foolish and lowly.
> "He wouldn't believe me if I told him.
> He wouldn't believe that I am his
>   father."

Outline:

> L3. Verses of sending
>
> people after him.
>
> M1. Verses of
>
> sending people.

Commentary:

HE THEN COMMANDED HIS ATTENDANTS/ TO SEIZE HIM AND
BRING HIM BACK/ "See that person?" he said, speaking of
his son, "Go get him and bring him back here." THE POOR
SON CRIED OUT IN ALARM/ This is exactly what he was afraid
would happen! They were coming after him! "What are you
doing? Why are you seizing me? I haven't committed any
crime! Are you going to kill me? I haven't broken any
laws! I wouldn't mind working for you, but I insist on
a salary." AND FAINTED, FALLING TO THE GROUND/ He was so
scared, he fainted. Those of the Two Vehicles did not understand the Great Vehicle and wondered why they were being forced to study it. "THESE PEOPLE HAVE CAUGHT ME/ I
SHALL CERTAINLY BE KILLED/ WHY, FOR FOOD AND CLOTHING'S
SAKE/ DID I COME TO THIS PLACE?"/ "They are going to kill
me for sure. What shall I do? If they kill me, I won't
be able to keep on eating and wearing clothes. Rats! Why
are you forcing me to go with you?"

THE ELDER KNEW THAT HIS SON/ WAS STUPID AND LOWLY/
He knew that his son was used to hanging around with poor
people and that he had never been to school, that he was

stupid and base, that he had no wisdom at all. In fact,
he was rotten. Because the son was so unintelligent, the
Elder knew that "HE WOULDN'T BELIEVE ME IF I TOLD HIM/
He would think I was trying to cheat him. If I told him
the truth, he would never believe me. HE WOULDN'T BE-
LIEVE THAT I AM HIS FATHER"/ So the father had lost his
son. The son was poor, and the father very rich; he
would never believe that he was his father. The father
uses his wisdom to think up an expedient device. If he
had told the boy directly that he was his father, the
poor son would not have believed him. The son had been
away too long, you see, and so he just couldn't have believed him.

Someone says, "The son ran away, and so now he does
not recognize his father. The father recognizes his son.
This happens all the time in the world."

True enough. However, this is no ordinary father
and son. This is a "transcendental," not a worldly, father. This is the great, compassionate father. He is
genuinely compassionate towards all living beings. "Genuine compassion" means that he is not the slightest bit selfish. Most fathers are kind to their children, but they
are more or less selfish about it. They think, "When I
get old, my children will take care of me."

"Dharma Master," you say, "this doesn't apply to
Americans. We don't hang on to our children, and when we

get old, we have Social Security!" So it is with worldy
parents.

The Buddha is our transcendental father. He wishes
to cross living beings over to Buddhahood. The poor son,
who is he? All living beings, all those of the Two Vehicles. They don't recognize their father. They run
away and get caught up in the bitter sea of birth and
death, bobbing up and down--birth and death, death and
birth, birth and death--so many times! And they don't
know how or why they are born, or how or why they die.
Muddled, they are born, and all messed up they die. They
may work all their lives to get their Ph.D.s, but not
long after they get them, they die! Once they die, they
forget everything they learned in school. They get reborn and have to start all over again! They go through
the whole thing again, and--sure enough--not long afterwards, they die. They work so hard to cram all those
things in their brains, and then they die and forget them
all again. What can be done?

The Buddha teaches us how to bring an end to the process of birth and death, to understand how it is we are
born and how it is that we die. He wants us to know why
some people are rich and others are poor, why some are
beautiful and others ugly. How does all this happen?
Who arranges it? Is it the parents? But parents don't
consciously plan their children's appearance or fate. The

Buddha tells us about ignorance conditioning activity,
conditioning consciousness, conditioning name and form,
and so on, all the Twelve Links. He wants us to wake up
from our confused dreams. But, as children we have run
away from our father. The Buddha is the father of all
living beings. But we would rather be poor sons, and we
don't want to return home. The Buddha recognizes his
children, but they do not recognize him. It's a predica-
ment, for sure. What's to be done?

Sutra: T. 8 a 16
Then he used an expedient,
And sent some other men,
One-eyed, squat, and ugly,
Lacking awesome virtue.
"Speak to him," he said,
"And tell him, 'You will work with
us
Getting rid of dung and filth
At twice your normal wages.'"
When the poor son heard this,
He happily followed them back
And swept out the dung and filth,
Cleaning all the dwellings.

Outline:

M2. Verses of sending

two people.

N1. Verses of in-

structions to work.

Commentary:

THEN HE USED AN EXPEDIENT/ The Elder knew the workings of the poor son's mind. He knew his son was rather base and didn't think in lofty terms. If he had told him he was his father, he would never have believed him. Therefore, he used an expedient device AND SENT SOME OTHER MEN/ He sent some Bodhisattvas disguised as Sound Hearers and Conditioned Enlightened Ones. ONE-EYED, SQUAT, AND UGLY/ "One-eyed" represents those of the Two Vehicles who have the "petty wisdom of one-sided emptiness." "Squat" refers to those of the Two Vehicles as not having fathomed the source of the Real Mark. They do not seek out the dharma of the Real Mark. "Ugly" means that they have not perfected the adornments of the myriad forms of goodness. They were not attractive in appearance.

LACKING AWESOME VIRTUE/ Those of the Two Vehicles do not possess the Four Fear.essnesses, and so they are not "awesome." Because they do not have the Four Virtues of Nirvana, they are said to be without "virtue."

"SPEAK TO HIM," HE SAID/ "AND TELL HIM, 'YOU WILL WORK WITH US/ What will you do? GETTING RID OF DUNG AND FILTH/ AT TWICE YOUR NORMAL WAGES"/ If before you made five dollars a day, you will now make ten dollars a day! The doubling of wages means that those of the Two Vehicles will now have a chance to certify to the fruits of Arhatship: the first, second, third, and fourth and then practice the Bodhisattva Path.

WHEN THE POOR SON HEARD THIS/ HE HAPPILY FOLLOWED THEM BACK/ He was delighted. He went to work getting rid of dung. AND SWEPT OUT THE DUNG AND FILTH/ Swept out the delusions of views and the delusions of thought, CLEANING ALL THE DWELLINGS/ He cleaned them. The dwellings here refer to the six sense organs and the Five Skandhas. Ordinarily, the eyes get attached to forms, the ears get attached to sounds, the nose gets attached to smells, and the tongue gets attached to tastes, the body gets attached to objects of touch, and the mind gets attached to dharmas. This attachment to the objects of sense makes one "unclean." Now, in cleaning the dwellings of the six senses, they have all been purified so that the eyes are not turned by forms, the ears are not turned by sounds, the nose is not turned by smells, the tongue is not turned by tastes, the body is not turned by objects of touch, and the mind does not get turned by dharmas. If you can purify the six sense organs, you are able to "turn states," instead of being turned by them. The Five Skandhas are also purified.

Sutra: T. 18a20

> From his window, the elder
> Would often watch his son,
> Remembering that he was foolish and
>   lowly
> And enjoyed menial work.
> Then the elder
> Put on a worn and dirty robe,
> And, holding a dung shovel,
> Went to where his son was.
> Expediently drawing near to him,
> He said, "Work with diligence,
> For I have increased your wages,
> And shall give you oil for your feet,
> And your fill of food and drink,
> And thick, warm bedding."
> Thus he spoke sharply saying,
> "You must work hard!"
> And then in gentler tones, he added,
> "You are like my own son."

Outline:

N2. Verses of

encouragement.

Commentary:

FROM HIS WINDOW, THE ELDER/ WOULD OFTEN WATCH HIS
SON/ REMEMBERING THAT HE WAS STUPID AND LOWLY/ too stupid!
AND ENJOYED MENIAL WORK/ He wouldn't cultivate the Great
Vehicle Dharma; he preferred to cultivate the Small Ve-
hicle.

THEN THE ELDER/ PUT ON A WORN AND DIRTY ROBE/ The
Buddha first spoke the <u>Great</u> <u>Avatamsaka</u> <u>Sutra</u>. At that

老人出家

賢愚因緣經云王舍城有長者名尸利
苾提其年百歲聞說出家功德無量便
自思惟我今何不於佛法中出家修道
往到竹園問諸比丘佛世尊今何所在
答言不在又問大師上足是誰比丘指
舍利弗詣前白言聽我出家舍利弗視
此老人三事皆缺不能學問坐禪助營
眾事告言汝去汝老不得出家次向大
迦葉優波離阿㝹樓陀五百大阿羅漢
等皆言年老不得出家遂出竹園住立
門外悲泣懊惱舉聲大哭世尊即至其
前放大光明相好端嚴佛問老人汝何
故哭長者聞佛梵音心懷喜躍如子見
父五體投地泣曰佛言我獨何罪不聽
出家佛言誰作是說年老不聽出家答
言舍利弗等爾時世尊以大慈悲慰諭
長者汝莫憂苦惱惟我能令汝得出
家非舍利弗次來隨我便隨佛俊入佛
精舍告大目連令與出家俊亦得證阿
羅漢果

The Buddha grants the old man permission to leave home.
(See The Amitabha Sutra, BTTS, 1974, p.21)

度弟難陀

寶藏經云佛至難陀舍乞食難陀作禮
取鉢盛飯奉佛佛不受鉢隨佛至精舍
佛遣難陀剃頭難陀恒欲還家佛不聽
許待佛來出去異道而歸佛不
遂見佛來大樹後藏佛即乘樹在空佛
見難陀將還精舍佛將難陀至忉利天
上遍諸天宮觀看見一宮中有諸天女
無有天子難陀出家終當生於此天宮
難陀便欲即住天女告言我等是天汝
子答言難陀遂問何以此宮獨無天
今是人還捨人妻更生此間佛將難陀
復至地獄見諸鑊湯慈沸人唯見一
鑊炊沸空停難陀即問獄卒答言難陀
以出家功德當得生天以欲罷道命終
墮此地獄是故我今炊鑊而待難陀恐
怖長獄辛留即作是言南無佛陀願佛
擁護將我還至精舍佛語難陀汝勤持
戒修汝天福難陀答言不用生天唯願
我莫墮此地獄佛與說法三七日中成
阿羅漢

The Buddha saves Sundarananda (See The Dharma Flower
Sutra, BTTS 1977, Vol.II,p.120)

time, those of the Two Vehicles had eyes but did not see him; they had ears but did not hear him. So the Buddha hid away the great and manifested the small. He hid away the great body with which he had spoken The Avatamsaka, and manifested instead in the body of an ordinary-sized Bhikshu. Manifesting as the old Bhikshu is represented in the text by "put on a worn and dirty robe."

AND, HOLDING A DUNG SHOVEL/ He manifested as one of the Two Vehicles, WENT TO WHERE HIS SON WAS/ The Buddha couldn't approach them directly, so he employed various expedients, EXPEDIENTLY DRAWING NEAR TO HIM/ HE SAID, "WORK WITH DILIGENCE"/ He exhorted him to cultivate the Four Applications of Mindfulness:

1. Contemplate the body as impure.

2. Contemplate feelings as suffering.

3. Contemplate thought as impermanent.

4. Contemplate dharmas as devoid of "self."

He also exhorted him to cultivate the Four Right Efforts:

1. Good that has not arisen is caused to arise.

2. Good that has arisen is caused to grow.

3. Evil that has not arisen is not allowed
   to arise.

4. Evil that has arisen is dispensed with.

"FOR I HAVE INCREASED YOUR WAGES/ This refers to the Four Bases of Psychic Power. AND SHALL GIVE YOU OIL FOR YOUR FEET/ Oil provides wind-proofing and water-proofing

for the feet. It provides Dhyana samadhis. YOUR FILL
OF FOOD AND DRINK/ The food and drink of spiritual penetrations. The food and drink refers to the rice, flour,
salt, and vinegar mentioned in the prose section. The
rice represents the emptiness of people. The flour represents the emptiness of dharmas. Rice and flour refer
to the Proper Path. Salt represents impermanence. Vinegar represents suffering. These two refer to the Aids to
the Path. If you want to eat rice or flour, you must add
some salt or vinegar to make them palatable. The Proper
Path, in the same way, needs the Aids of the Path for
"flavoring."

"AND THICK, WARM BEDDING"/ This represents the continued contemplations cultivated in the practice of Dhyana samadhi.

THUS, HE SPOKE SHARPLY SAYING/ "YOU MUST WORK HARD!"/
Do not be lazy. Work hard and don't waste your time.
Cultivate the Four Right Efforts and the Four Bases of
Psychic Power.

AND THEN IN GENTLER TONES, HE ADDED/ in reassuring
tones,"YOU ARE LIKE MY OWN SON"/ Work hard. Don't get
distracted. Don't strike up false thinking; don't run
away. Just stay here and keep working. You are just like
my very own son."

Sutra: T. 18a26
>
> The elder, in his wisdom,
> Eventually allowed him to come
>   and go.
> For a period of twenty years,
> He was put in charge of household
>   business.
> He showed him his gold, silver,
> Real pearls and crystal.
> The income and expense of all
>   these things,
> He was caused to know.
> And yet the son still lived outside
>   the gate,
> Dwelling in a grass hut
> Thinking of his poverty:
> "None of these things are mine."

Outline:

> L4. Verses of passing on
>
> the inheritance.
>
>> M1. The inheritance.

Commentary:

THE ELDER, IN HIS WISDOM/ The Buddha, in his wisdom,
teaches and transforms all living beings, causing all
living beings to turn from the Two Vehicles and understand the Great Vehicle Dharma. EVENTUALLY ALLOWS HIM
TO COME AND GO/ to go back and forth from the Two Vehicles to the Great Vehicle. FOR A PERIOD OF TWENTY YEARS/
In cultivation, it took twenty years to get rid of the

dung of delusions of views and thought. HE WAS PUT IN
CHARGE OF THE HOUSEHOLD BUSINESS/ During that twenty
years, he was in charge of all the affairs of the Elder's
household. HE SHOWED HIM HIS GOLD, SILVER/ REAL PEARLS,
AND CRYSTAL/ THE INCOME AND EXPENSE OF ALL HIS THINGS/
his valuables. HE WAS CAUSED TO KNOW/ all the Buddha's
dharmas, those of the Two Vehicles were led to understand.
AND YET THE SON STILL LIVED OUTSIDE THE GATE/ Even though
the poor son was in charge of all the valuables, he still
stayed outside the gate. Those of the Two Vehicles remained outside. They did not enter the gateway of the
Great Vehicle. DWELLING IN A GRASS HUT/ in a small cottage. The small grass hut represents the state of the
Two Vehicles. THINKING OF HIS POVERTY/ Those of the Two
Vehicles thought of themselves as such. They thought
that the teaching and transforming of living beings, the
purification of Buddhalands--those activites of the Bod-
hisattvas--had nothing to do with them. The Great Vehicle Buddhadharma was not too important to them. "NONE
OF THESE THINGS ARE MINE."

Sutra: T.18 b 1
> The father knew his son's mind
> Gradually had expanded,
> And wishing to give him wealth,
> He gathered together his relatives,
> The kings, and great ministers,
> The kshatriyas and laypeople.
> In the midst of this great assembly,
> He said, "This is my son.
> He left me and went away
> Fifty years ago.
> And it has been twenty years
> Since I saw him return.
> Long ago in a certain city
> I lost my son.
> Searching for him everywhere,
> I came to this place.
> Everything that I own,
> My houses and servants,
> I bequeath it all to him
> That he may use it as he pleases."

Outline:

> M2. Verses of be-
> queathing.
>> N1. Verses of
>> bequeathing
>> proper.

Commentary:

THE FATHER KNEW HIS SON'S MIND/ GRADUALLY HAD EXPAN-
DED/ After a time, the son no longer lacked self-respect.
His mind was larger, AND WISHING TO GIVE HIM HIS WEALTH/

The Buddha wished to give all his Buddhadharma to those of the Two Vehicles. HE GATHERED TOGETHER HIS RELATIVES/ THE KINGS, AND GREAT MINISTERS/ all the great Bodhisattvas. THE KSHATRIYAS AND LAYPEOPLE/ IN THE MIDST OF THIS GREAT ASSEMBLY/ HE SAID, "THIS IS MY SON/ HE LEFT ME AND WENT AWAY/ When just a child he ran off to another country, FIFTY YEARS AGO/ He fell into the wheel of rebirth of the five paths in the Three Realms. AND IT HAS BEEN TWENTY YEARS/ SINCE I SAW HIM RETURN/ Those of the Two Vehicles had heard the Great Vehicle Dharma before. They had forgotten it, all right, but it was still there floating around in their subconscious, as it were. They had been cultivating, now, for twenty years, working at sweeping out the dung, practicing the Bodhisattva-dharmas.

"LONG AGO IN A CERTAIN CITY/ I LOST MY SON/ SEARCHING FOR HIM EVERYWHERE/ I CAME TO THIS PLACE/ EVERYTHING THAT I OWN/ MY HOUSES AND SERVANTS/ I BEQUEATH IT ALL TO HIM/ THAT HE MAY USE IT AS HE PLEASES/ He can do whatever he wants with it." The Buddha turns over his entire inheritance of the Buddhadharma to those of the Two Vehicles as something that was rightfully theirs all along.

Sutra: T.18b8
> The son, recalling his former pov
> erty
> And his lowly intentions,
> Who now, in his father's presence
> Had obtained these precious jewels,

And these dwelling places,
And all such wealth,
Greatly rejoiced,
Having gained what he'd never had.

Outline:

> N2. Verses of
>
> rejoicing.

Commentary:

THE SON, RECALLING HIS FORMER POVERTY/ Those of the
Two Vehicles are interested in self-improvement only. AND
HIS LOWLY INTENTIONS/ He had no great resolve, no great
ambitions. WHO NOW IN HIS FATHER'S PRESENCE/ HAD OBTAINED
THESE PRECIOUS JEWELS/ AND THESE DWELLING PLACES/ AND ALL
SUCH WEALTH/ GREATLY REJOICED/ HAVING GAINED WHAT HE'D
NEVER HAD/

Sutra: 18 b11
The Buddha in the same way
Knew our fondness for the petty.

Outline:

> K2. Verses correlated
> with Dharma.
>
> > L1. Correlating the
> > separation and meet-
> > ing.

1008

Commentary:

THE BUDDHA IN THE SAME WAY/ KNEW OUR FONDNESS FOR THE
PETTY/ He knew that we preferred the small vehicle.

Sutra: T. 18b12
   And so he never said to us,
   "You shall become Buddhas."
   Instead he said that we
   Could attain cessation of all outflows,
   Realize the lesser vehicle,
   And become Sound Hearer Disciples.

Outline:

L2. Correlating send-

                                        ing people after him.

Commentary:

AND SO HE NEVER SAID TO US/ He never told us that we,
the Sound Hearers, could become Buddhas. "YOU SHALL BE-
COME BUDDHAS"/

INSTEAD HE SAID THAT WE/ COULD ATTAIN THE CESSATION
OF ALL OUTFLOWS/ He said that we might attain the cessation of outflows, that is, the Nirvana with Residue of
the small vehicle. Those of the Sound Hearer Vehicle
awaken to the Way when they hear the sound of the Buddha's voice speaking the Dharma. Thus, they REALIZE THE
LESSER VEHICLE/ AND BECOME SOUND HEARER DISCIPLES/

Sutra: T. 18b13

    The Buddha has instructed us
To speak of the unsurpassed Path,
And spoken of those who practice it
As being able to accomplish Buddha-
    hood.
Receiving the Buddha's teaching, we
For the sake of the Great Bodhisattvas,
Use causes and conditions,
Various analogies,
And numerous expressions
To speak of the unsurpassed Path.
All the Buddha's disciples,
Having heard from us this Dharma,
Think upon it day and night,
And diligently practice it.
Thereupon, all the Buddhas,
Then bestow predictions upon them,
Saying, "You, in a future age,
Shall become Buddhas."
This is the secret store of Dharma,
Of all the Buddhas.
Only for the Bodhisattvas
Are such real matters set forth.
And not for our sakes
Have such true essentials been
    spoken.

Outline:

        L3. Correlating the
        inheritance.

          M1. Correlating
          the inheritance
          proper.

Commentary:

THE BUDDHA HAS INSTRUCTED US/ TO SPEAK OF THE UNSUR-
PASSED PATH/ AND OF THOSE WHO PRACTICE IT/ AS BEING ABLE
TO ACCOMPLISH BUDDHAHOOD/ Those who practice the Great
Vehicle will eventually accomplish the ultimate Buddha-
fruit. RECEIVING THE BUDDHA'S TEACHING WE/ FOR THE SAKE
OF THE GREAT BODHISATTVAS/ USE CAUSES AND CONDITIONS/
VARIOUS ANALOGIES/ AND NUMEROUS EXPRESSIONS/ TO SPEAK THE
UNSURPASSED PATH/

ALL THE BUDDHA'S DISCIPLES/ HAVING HEARD FROM US THIS
DHARMA/ THINK UPON IT DAY AND NIGHT/ AND DILIGENTLY PRAC-
TICE IT/ THEREUPON, ALL THE BUDDHAS/ THEN BESTOW PREDIC-
TIONS UPON THEM/ SAYING, "YOU, IN A FUTURE AGE/ SHALL BE-
COME BUDDHAS"/ Then, all the Buddhas, with the same sound,
seal and certify this fact by bestowing predictions of future Buddhahood upon the Bodhisattvas. They say, "You,
in limitless ages hence, will perfect the Bodhisattva path
and become Buddhas."

THIS IS THE SECRET STORE OF DHARMA/ OF ALL THE BUD-
DHAS/ the secret Dharma-jewel of all the Buddhas throughout the ten directions. ONLY FOR THE BODHISATTVAS/ ARE
SUCH REAL MATTERS SET FORTH/ It is only for those with the
potential of the Great Vehicle Bodhisattvas, that such
subtle, wonderful, true matters are expounded. AND NOT

FOR OUR SAKES/ HAVE SUCH TRUE ESSENTIALS BEEN SPOKEN/ It's
not for the small vehicle people that such real Dharma
has been taught. The provisional Dharma was spoken for
those of the small vehicle. The real Dharma was not spoken for them.

Sutra: T. 18b21

> Just as the poor son
> Drew near his father, and
> Although he knew of all his posses-
> sions,
> In his heart he held no hope of get-
> ting them,
> In just the same way,
> Even though we have spoken
> Of the Buddhadharma's precious
> store,
> We personally never aspired to it.

Outline:

> N2. Correlating
> lack of aspira-
> tion.
>> O1. Correlat-
>> ing general
>> lack of hope.

Commentary:

JUST AS THE POOR SON/ DREW NEAR HIS FATHER, AND/ AL-
THOUGH HE KNEW OF ALL HIS POSSESSIONS/ IN HIS HEART HE
HELD NO HOPE OF GETTING THEM/ He knew of all his father's

valuables, but it never occurred to him to call these
things his own. IN JUST THE SAME WAY/ EVEN THOUGH WE HAVE
SPOKEN/ We of the small vehicle have spoken OF THE BUDDHA
DHARMA'S PRECIOUS STORE/ WE'VE PERSONALLY NEVER ASPIRED
FOR IT/ We felt there was no point in seeking the Great
Vehicle Dharma of the Bodhisattvas. The poor son knew
of all the treasures, yet he did not know that they belonged to him. He still held on to his small viewpoint
and didn't expand his thinking. Now, he finally understands that we all have a share in the Buddha's wealth.

Sutra: T. 18 b 24

Having attained inner-extinction,
We thought this sufficient,
For having completed this,
There was nothing else to be done.
And even if we had heard
Of purifying Buddhalands,
And teaching and transforming
living beings,
We'd have taken no delight therein.
And for what reason?
All dharmas are
Completely empty and still,
Neither produced nor destroyed,
Neither great nor small,
Without outflows and uncondi-
tioned.
Reflecting in this way,
We did not give rise to joy.
During the long night,

We had no craving or attachment
For the Buddha's wisdom,
Nor did we aspire to it.
Yet, as to Dharma, we
Claimed we had the ultimate.
All through the long night,
We practiced and cultivated the
      Dharma of emptiness.
Having won release from the
      triple world
With its suffering, distress and
      calamites,
We dwell within our final bodies,
In nirvana with residue.
According to the Buddha's teaching,
We attained the Way which is not
      false,
And we assumed that we had
Thereby repaid the Buddha's
      kindness.

Outline:

02. Correlat-

ing explain-

ing no hope.

Commentary:

Mahakashyapa says that, HAVING ATTAINED INNER EXTINC-

TION/ We who cultivate the Two Vehicles have already got-

ten rid of the false thinking within ourselves. This ab-

sence of false thinking is what is called "inner-extinc-

tion." And WE THOUGHT THIS SUFFICIENT/ Because we had no

false thinking, we thought that we were always in samadhi. We felt that with "one thought not produced, the entire substance manifests." The state in which not a single thought arises is called "inner-extinction." WE THOUGHT THIS SUFFICIENT/ We felt that this was enough. We had cultivated to the point that we had no more false thinking. FOR, HAVING COMPLETED THIS/ THERE WAS NOTHING ELSE TO BE DONE/ or so we thought. We have already cut off our afflictions and broken through our ignorance, so that we are always giving rise to inner-wisdom. So what else is there to be done?

AND EVEN IF WE HAD HEARD/ OF PURIFYING BUDDHALANDS/ of purifying and adorning the Buddhalands, of turning from the small vehicle towards the Great Vehicle, and of practicing the Bodhisattva path and teaching and transforming living beings, AND OF TEACHING AND TRANSFORMING LIVING BEINGS/ of enlightening oneself and others, of benefitting oneself and others, and leading all living beings to understand the Buddhadharma, WE'D HAVE TAKEN NO DELIGHT THEREIN/ We would have thought, "That's asking too much. Can't we just cultivate, gain our own attainment and then forget it? What's with going around teaching everybody else? That's really just making up things to keep yourself busy!" Those of the Two Vehicles are independent. They work for their own accomplishment and don't care to worry about other people. "Who cares if they fall into the hells or turn into animals? Let them do what they like! I'm enlightened already, and they are simply none of my business! I have broken through ignorance and seen the Dharma nature, and I don't care about saving living beings." They are not the least bit interested in purifying the Buddhalands and teaching living beings.

AND FOR WHAT REASON?/ ALL DHARMAS ARE/ COMPLETELY EMPTY AND STILL/ They are empty! What's the big deal about teaching living beings?

Although all Dharmas are empty and still, one still must practice the Bodhisattva path and benefit others. But those of the Two Vehicles are lazy, they don't want to do this. They hold to the saying,

Mahasattvas don't watch over others.

And Amitabha Buddha takes care of himself. Your suffering is your business. I have some skill, and so I don't suffer. That's good enough for me. Your suffering is none of my business. Basically, all the Buddhas and all living beings are one. The Buddha is living beings, and living beings are the Buddha. Those of the Two Vehicles have arrived at "Transformation City," and they like it there just fine. They were once vigorous in pursuit of the Way, but having arrived half-way, they grow lazy. "I've gotten quite enough." This is like people who are quite vigorous in their cultivation before they leave the home-life. But, once they have left home, they think, "I have already received the precepts. It doesn't matter anymore whether or not I cultivate. I can keep my old bad habits, and if I get a little lazy, it's no problem." That's just the way those of the Two Vehicles are. They have cultivated and attained some benefits, and having rid themselves of ignorance and affliction, they think, "This is really wonderful." They end up enjoying how "wonderful" everything is for them, and they don't think to teach and transform living beings, to purify the Buddhalands. They take no delight in such ideas. Why not? Everything is empty and still. If they felt delighted they would just be getting attached again! What they don't realize is that their passivity is also a form of attachment! Hah! Delight and non-delight are both attachments!

ALL DHARMAS ARE/ COMPLETELY EMPTY AND STILL/ NEITHER PRODUCED NOR DESTROYED/ NEITHER GREAT NOR SMALL/ They think, "Since all dharmas aren't produced or destroyed, why should I bring about production and extinction?" WITHOUT OUTFLOWS AND UNCONDITIONED/ REFLECTING IN THIS WAY/ WE DID NOT GIVE RISE TO JOY/ They aren't interested in practicing the Bodhisattva's path, in purifying the Buddhalands, in teaching and transforming living beings. They find the whole idea to be a pain in the neck!

WE, DURING THE LONG NIGHT/ During the long night of

time, WE HAD NO CRAVING OR ATTACHMENT/ FOR THE BUDDHA'S
WISDOM/ We did not covet even the wisdom of the Buddha,
that bright light which illumines the dark night of time.
We had no attachments. Above, we felt there was no Buddhahood for us to realize, and below there were no living
beings to save. We had no hope of becoming Buddhas, and
we had no wisdom to save living beings. I don't know
quite what we thought we were doing! We weren't doing
anything, in fact!" And you wonder why the Buddha scolded
those of the Two Vehicles calling them withered sprouts
and sterile seeds? They weren't reaching for Buddhahood;
they weren't teaching living beings. They were exactly
nowhere; they were drying up and blowing away. They did
not even care about attaining the Buddha's wisdom or becoming a Buddha, NOR DID WE ASPIRE TO IT/ It didn't figure
in their plans at all.

AND YET, AS TO DHARMA, WE/ CLAIMED WE HAD THE ULTI-
MATE/ We thought we had achieved inner-extinction, broken
through ignorance and severed affliction, and we thought
that was about all there was to cultivation. We have no
afflictions or ignorance. You can scold us or hit us,
and it doesn't matter. This is the ultimate in all Dharmas. ALL THROUGH THE LONG NIGHT/ WE PRACTICED AND CULTI-
VATED THE DHARMA OF EMPTINESS/ We have cut off affliction
in the Three Realms. HAVING WON RELEASE FROM THE TRIPLE
WORLD/ WITH ITS SUFFERING, DISTRESS, AND CALAMITIES/ WE

DWELL WITHIN OUR FINAL BODIES/ and we do not again have
to undergo birth and death IN NIRVANA WITH RESIDUE/ AC-
CORDING TO THE BUDDHA'S TEACHING/ WE ATTAINED THE WAY
WHICH IS NOT FALSE/ We have attained the fruits of the
Path. AND WE ASSUMED THAT WE HAD/ THEREBY REPAID THE
BUDDHA'S KINDNESS/ We thought that our attainment of the
nirvana with residue and our certification to the Fourth
Fruit of Arhatship was, in fact, repaying the Buddha's
kindness." But it wasn't, really, because those of the
Two Vehicles did not cultivate the Bodhisattva Path, did
not adorn the Buddhalands and did not teach and transform
living beings. All they cared about was #1, and that
doesn't count as repaying the Buddha's kindness.

Sutra: T. 18c6
> Although we, for the sake
> Of the Buddha's disciples spoke
> Of the Bodhisattvas Dharma,
> With which they should seek
>   Buddhahood,
> Still in this Dharma,
> We never took delight at all.
> Our master saw this and let
>   things be,
> Because he saw into our hearts,
> And so, at first, he did not en-
>   courage us
> By telling of the real advantage.

Outline:

O3. Conclu-

sion.

Commentary:

ALTHOUGH WE, FOR THE SAKE/ OF THE BUDDHA'S DISCIPLES, SPOKE/ OF THE BODHISATTVA'S DHARMA/ WITH WHICH THEY SHOULD SEEK BUDDHAHOOD/ YET, IN THIS DHARMA/ WE NEVER TOOK DE-LIGHT AT ALL/ We never hoped for it ourselves; we were not the slightest bit interested in it. We didn't want to practice the Bodhisattva Path. We were satisfied with the little we had; we felt happy enough at having arrived in Transformation City. We weren't greedy for Buddhahood. Above, we felt no need to realize Buddhahood, and below we had no interest in teaching living beings.

OUR MASTER SAW THIS AND LET THINGS BE/ The Buddha knew that we didn't want to cultivate the Great Vehicle Buddhadharma, and so he didn't speak the Great Vehicle Buddhadharma to us, BECAUSE HE SAW INTO OUR HEARTS/ He knew that we liked the small vehicle. AND SO, AT FIRST, HE DID NOT ENCOURAGE US/ BY TELLING US OF THE REAL ADVAN-TAGE/ In the beginning he just taught us about the Four Holy Truths and the Twelve Causal Conditions. He didn't encourage us to practice the Six Perfections and Ten Thousand Conducts of the Bodhisattva. He didn't tell us to practice the Bodhisattva path and become Buddhas. He merely encouraged us to attain the Four Fruits of Arhat-ship."

Sutra: T.18c9
>Just as the wealthy elder
>Used the power of expedients
>To bring his mind under control,
>And afterwards gave to him
>All of his valuables,
>The Buddha in the same way
>Manifests rare things,
>But for those who delight in the
>   small,
>He uses the power of expedients
>To bring their minds under control,
>Only then teaching the greater
>   wisdom.

Outline:

> M2. Correlating be-
> queathing the in-
> heritance.

>> N1. Correlating
>> the bequeathing.

Commentary:

JUST AS THE WEALTHY ELDER/ KNOWS HIS SON'S LOWLY AM-
BITIONS/ knowing he had no lofty resolve, USED THE POWER
OF EXPEDIENTS/ used various expedient methods, TO BRING
HIS MIND UNDER CONTROL/ Bit by bit he tamed him, he drew
near him, chatted with him, he put on a worn and dirty
robe... This means that the Buddha manifested as an or-
dinary Bhikshu so that he could draw near to those of the
Two Vehicles. Gradually, he subdued their minds. AND

AFTERWARDS GAVE TO HIM/ ALL OF HIS VALUABLES/ THE BUDDHA, IN THE SAME WAY/ MANIFESTS RARE THINGS/ Things never seen before, dharmas never known before, BUT FOR THOSE WHO DELIGHT IN THE SMALL/ those of the Two Vehicles, he speaks the small vehicle dharma. HE USES THE POWER OF EXPEDIENTS/ TO BRING THEIR MINDS UNDER CONTROL/ And once their minds have been subdued, ONLY THEN TEACHING THE GREATER WISDOM/ only then are they receptive to the Great Vehicle Buddhadharma.

Sutra: T. 18c14

On this day, we
Have gained what we never had!
That for which we lacked hope,
We now have attained.
Just as the poor son
Gained limitless treasure,
O World Honored One, now
We've obtained the Path and its fruits.
Within the non-outflow Dharma
We've gained the eye, pure and clear.
During the long night, we
Maintained the Buddha's pure morality
But only on this day,
Have we gained this reward.
In the Dharma King's Dharma,
Long have we cultivated Brahman conduct.
Now we've obtained that non-outflow,
The unsurpassed, great fruition.

Now we are all
Truly Sound Hearers.
And taking the sound of the Buddha's
    Way,
We cause all to hear it.
Now we are all
Truly Arhats,
And in all the world,
With its gods, people, maras and
    Brahmas,
Everywhere among them
We are worthy of receiving offerings.

Outline:

N2. Correlating

the rejoicing.

Commentary:

ON THIS DAY, WE/ HAVE GAINED WHAT WE NEVER HAD/ THAT
FOR WHICH WE LACKED HOPE/ WE NOW HAVE ATTAINED/ JUST AS
THE POOR SON/ GAINED LIMITLESS TREASURES/ Basically, he
had no idea he would be bequeathed all of his father's
wealth.

WORLD HONORED ONE, NOW/ WE'VE OBTAINED THE PATH AND
ITS FRUITS/ the fruition of the unsurpassed Buddha Path.
WITHIN THE NON-OUTFLOW DHARMA/ WE'VE GAINED THE EYE, PURE
AND CLEAR/ We've gained the clear, pure Buddha-eye and
opened the wisdom of the Buddha.

DUIRNG THE LONG NIGHT, WE/ MAINTAINED THE BUDDHA'S
PURE MORALITY/ During the long night of time, we have up-

held the pure, precious precepts of the Buddha. BUT ONLY
ON THIS DAY/ HAVE WE GAINED THIS REWARD/ IN THE DHARMA
KING'S DHARMA/ In the Buddhadharma LONG HAVE WE CULTIVA-
TED BRAHMAN CONDUCT/ We have been practicing pure conduct
for a long, long time, for over forty years, now. NOW
WE'VE OBTAINED THAT NON-OUTFLOW/ THE UNSURPASSED GREAT
FRUITION/ and there is nothing higher than this position.
NOW WE ARE ALL/ TRULY SOUND HEARERS/ AND TAKING THE SOUND
OF THE BUDDHA'S WAY/ WE CAUSE ALL TO HEAR IT/ so that
all living beings get to hear the Buddhadharma. NOW WE
ARE ALL/ TRULY ARHATS/ we are "Slayers of Thieves," "Ones
Worthy of Offerings," "Ones Not Born." AND IN ALL THE
WORLD/ WITH ITS GODS, PEOPLE, MARAS, AND BRAHMANS/ EVERY-
WHERE AMONG THEM/ WE ARE WORTHY OF RECEIVING OFFERINGS/
We are truly worthy of receiving their offerings within
the Triple Realm.

For those who have left home, it is not easy to accept the offerings of those who have not left home. It
is said, "If you haven't ended the three phases of thought,
you'll find plain water hard to digest." The three phases of thought refer to past thought, present thought,
and future thought. The Diamond Sutra says, "Past thought
cannot be got at; present thought cannot be got at; future thought cannot be got at." But have you got at it?
As to the past, it has already gone by and cannot be obtained. The present is just now becoming the past, and

it doesn't stand still. The future simply hasn't come
yet. One may make verbal reference to the three phases
of thought as unobtainable, but on a more practical level. have you ended the three phases of thought? Do you
think about the past? Have you forgotten what happened
in the past? No? Then you have "obtained" past thought.
Is your thought at present empty? Are you running thoughts
through your head concerning your next shopping trip? Or
your next project? There! You have "obtained" present
thought. Are you planning for your future? You have
just "obtained" future thought! See? If you have no
thought of the past, no thoughts in the present, and no
concern for the future, then you can say, "The three phases of thought cannot be obtained." It should be the
case that you,

> Sweep away the three phases of thought,
>
> And separate from all marks.

But, if as a left-home person you have not ended the three
phases of thought, you are going to have trouble trying
to digest a cup of water, to say nothing of digesting your
lunch!

> Back to the saying,
>
> > If you haven't ended the three phases of
> > thought, you'll find plain water hard
> > to digest.
>
> But, if you've understood the Five Contem-

plations,

You'll be able to digest metal!

I've noticed lately that there is a lot of chatter going on at the lunch table. Probably you have all forgotten the Five Contemplations. You <u>should</u> forget the Three Phases of Thought, but you can't forget them! You should remember the Five Contemplations, but you can't remember them!

What are the Five Contemplations, then?

1. Consider the amount of work it took to get the food to you.

2. Consider whether you have enough merit to accept the offering.

3. Guard your mind against offenses such as greed.

In other words, don't get greedy when you see good things to eat, and don't get disgusted when the food's not good. You should be even-minded regardless of what's on the table.

4. Remember the food is only medicine, to prevent the body from going bad.

Eating food is just like taking medicine. You shouldn't get caught up in the taste of food. It is taken merely to keep you going.

5. I only take this food in order to realize the karma of the Way.

I eat so that I may live, and I live so that I may culti-

vate and realize the Way.

So, the text says, WE ARE WORTHY OF RECEIVING OF-

FERINGS.

Sutra: T. 18c21

 The World Honored One in his great kind-
   ness,
 Uses this rare thing,
 To pity, teach,
 And benefit us,
 Throughout limitless millions of aeons.
 Who could repay him?
 Giving one's hands and feet,
 Bowing reverently in obeisance,
 Whatever offering one makes,
 Never repays him.
 If one bore him on one's head,
 Or carried him upon one's shoulders,
 For aeons as numerous as the Ganges'
   sands,
 Exhausting one's mind in reverence—
 Or further, if one used delicacies,
 And limitless valuable clothing,
 And all types of bedding,
 And various medicines,
 Ox-head sandalwood,
 And various precious gems,
 Or Stupas and temples
 Covering the ground with valuable
   cloth,
 And if with such things as these,
 One made offerings

Throughout aeons as numerous as
 the Ganges' sands,
One still never repays him.
The Buddhas are rare indeed.
Limitless and boundless,
Yes, inconceivable is the power,
Of their great spiritual penetrations.
Without outflows, unconditioned,
They are Kings of all the Dharmas.
For the sake of lesser beings,
They bear up under this work.
To common folks who grasp at marks,
They teach what is appropriate.
The Buddhas have, within the Dharmas,
Attained to the highest comfort.
They understand all living beings'
Various desires and delights,
As well as the strength of their re-
 solve,
According to what they can bear,
Using limitless analogies,
They teach them the Dharma,
In accord with living beings'
Wholesome roots from former lives.
And knowing those who have
 matured,
And those who have not yet
 matured,
Through such calculations,
They discriminate and understand,
And in the pathway of One Vehicle,
They appropriately speak of three.

Outline:

> H2. Verses in praise of the
> Buddha's kindness.

Commentary:

THE WORLD HONORED ONE, IN HIS GREAT KINDNESS/ USES THIS RARE THING/ employs the unsurpassed Dharma, which is extremely rare in the world, TO PITY, TEACH/ AND BENEFIT US/ In the Ten Dharma Realms he causes all living beings to make the Four Vast Vows and to accomplish the unsurpassed, wonderful fruition of Bodhi. He causes us to bring forth the Bodhi mind and eventually realize the wonderful fruit of enlightenment. This is the greatest form of kindness there is. He leads living beings to separate from suffering and attain bliss. THROUGHOUT LIMITLESS MILLIONS OF AEONS/ Living beings have forgotten the Great Vehicle Dharma. They take suffering as bliss. Although they have forgotten, the "seeds" of the power of their vows--these Great Vehicle seeds--do not get lost. So now the Buddha uses the power of his great compassion to bring happiness to all living beings. He leads all living beings to attain peace and comfort. Living beings undergoing suffering are like children being bullied who go running to their father. They can find no way out of it themselves, and so the Buddha teaches them the Six Perfections and the Ten Thousand Conducts. He teaches them the Bodhisattva Path of benefitting oneself and benefitting others,

so that in the future they can realize Buddhahood. After
the Buddha became a Buddha himself, he was basically en-
titled to enjoy the happiness of still extinction. He
didn't have to do anything else. But, the Buddha was unable to let go of living beings, and so he taught the Buddhadharma to all living beings. He taught them to keep
the five precepts, to practice the ten good deeds, and to
cultivate in accord with Dharma. First, he spoke The Great
Avatamsaka Sutra. But, because the potentials of living
beings had not yet matured sufficiently to understand the
doctrines of The Avatamsaka Sutra, the Buddha "hid away the
great and manifested the small." He manifested as an old
Bhikshu to draw near to all living beings. This was a manifestation of the Buddha's great compassion. He drew near
to living beings, and as they gradually got to know him
better, they grew to have faith in him. The Buddha bequeathed all of his valuables to the Two Vehicles; he turned
over his entire inheritance to them. He had a meeting, and
amidst all the great kings and ministers and householders,
he decided that his entire wealth would be turned over to
those of the Two Vehicles--they in the future can become
Buddhas. They will eventually sit on the Buddha's throne,
purify the Buddhalands, and teach and transform living beings. This just shows us the Buddha's great kindness.

HE USES THIS RARE THING/ this most rare Dharma, TO
PITY, TEACH/ AND BENEFIT US/ not just for a short while,

but THROUGHOUT LIMITLESS MILLIONS OF AEONS/ WHO COULD RE-
PAY HIM?/ The World Honored One has been so good to us.
How can we ever repay him?

GIVING ONE'S HANDS AND FEET/ BOWING REVERENTLY IN
OBEISANCE/ WHATEVER OFFERING ONE MAKES/ NEVER REPAYS HIM/
There is no way to repay the great kindness of the Buddha.
To offer one's hands and feet means to do work for the
Buddha.

IF ONE BORE HIM ON ONE'S HEAD/ OR CARRIED HIM UPON
ONE'S SHOULDERS/ FOR AEONS AS NUMEROUS AS THE GANGE'S
SANDS/ EXHAUSTING ONE'S MIND IN REVERENCE/ Doing abso-
lutely everything in one's power to show reverence and
respect, OR FURTHER, IF ONE USED DELICACIES/ AND LIMIT-
LESS VALUABLE CLOTHING/ AND ALL TYPES OF BEDDING/ AND
VARIOUS MEDICINES/ These are the four types of offerings:
food and drink, bedding, clothing, and medicines. OX-
HEAD SANDALWOOD/ AND VARIOUS PRECIOUS GEMS/ OR BUILT STUP-
AS AND TEMPLES/ COVERING THE GROUND WITH VALUABLE CLOTH/
AND IF WITH SUCH THINGS AS THESE/ ONE MADE OFFERINGS/
THROUGHOUT AEONS AS NUMEROUS AS THE GANGES' SANDS/
ONE STILL COULD NEVER REPAY HIM/

THE BUDDHAS ARE RARE, INDEED/ LIMITLESS AND BOUND-
LESS/ YES, INCONCEIVABLE IS THE POWER/ OF THEIR GREAT
SPIRITUAL PENETRATIONS/ There is no one else in the world
like the Buddha. The Buddha's state is limiteless and
boundless and inconceivable.

WITHOUT OUTFLOWS, UNCONDITIONED/ THEY ARE KINGS OF
ALL DHARMAS/ The Buddha has attained to the state of no-
outflows and certified to the wonderful doctrine of the
unconditioned. Therefore, within all the Dharmas he is
the King, his is the highest position, and yet FOR THE
SAKE OF LESSER BEINGS/ The Buddha will refrain from speaking the highest, Great Vehicle Buddhadharma, and for the
sake of the Real meanifest the Provisional. He will teach
the expedient devices for those inferior. THEY BEAR UP
UNDER THIS WORK/ With patience, they undertake to educate
those who are inferior by teaching them the provisional
doctrine.

TO COMMON FOLKS WHO GRASP AT MARKS/ THEY TEACH WHAT
IS APPROPRIATE/ They give the common folks what they like.
If they like what is sweet, they give them something sweet.
If they like what is salty, they give them something salty.
If they like hot, bitter, or sour things, they give them
what they like, according to their tastes. If they need
to be crossed over by means of bitter dharmas, they teach
them bitter dharmas. If they need to be crossed over by
means of joyful dharmas, they give them joyful dharmas.
If they need to be crossed over by means of kindness, they
teach them the dharmas of kindness. If they need to be
crossed over by means of compassionate dharmas, they teach
them compassionate dharmas. The Buddha cherishes and pro-
tects all living beings as one would love and protect

one's own children. He looks upon all living beings as
if they were his own children. He looks upon them as if
they were his own parents. So the Buddha said,

All men are like my father.

All women are like my mother.

Since all men are like one's father, one should be filial.
Seeing all women as like one's mother, one should also be
filial. If one has this attitude, one will not fall into
deviant knowledge and views regarding living beings. One
won't be prone to desire. The practice of filiality pre-
cludes lustful thoughts towards others. That is why the
Buddha treats all living beings as equals.

There is a saying,

If you wish to lead them into the Buddha's
wisdom,

You must first bait the hook with something
that they like.

Fishermen have to put some bait on their hooks, something
that the fish like to eat, and then the fish will bite,
and you can reel them in. If your relatives and friends
do not believe in the Buddhadharma, you can bring them
here to have a good lunch. If the food is good, they will
remember it and think about coming back at the next oppor-
tunity. You can say, "That lunch wasn't so good. I know
something that's even better. Try the Dharma! That's
even better." And then they hear the Dharma and get

crossed over.

THEY TEACH THEM WHAT IS APPROPRIATE/ They teach the right dharma at the right time. They teach them what they need to learn.

THE BUDDHAS HAVE, WITHIN THE DHARMAS/ ATTAINED TO THE HIGHEST COMFORT/ They are the freest and most at ease. They are "right-on" all the time.

THEY UNDERSTAND ALL LIVING BEINGS'/ VARIOUS DESIRES AND DELIGHTS/ Some like to hear the Buddhadharma; others like to go to movies. Some like to dance; others like tennis. Some like to sleep! Some like to eat! Some like to go jogging. Everybody's different. But, the Buddha knows what they like best, and knows AS WELL THE STRENGTH OF THEIR RESOLVE/ AND ACCORDING TO WHAT THEY CAN BEAR/ according to what they will accept, USING LIMITLESS ANALOGIES/ THEY TEACH THE DHARMA TO THEM/ IN ACCORD WITH LIVING BEINGS'/ WHOLESOME ROOTS FROM FORMER LIVES/ We living beings come into this world with different predilections. This life we are friends with one person, and in the next life we are friends with another. In this life, one person is our father, and in the next life, someone else takes that role. This life one is married to one person, and in the next life to another. Father/ son this life, father/son with another next life. One undergoes retribution according to karma created in former lives. We have come into this world to undergo retribution. So people shouldn't be so stupid. Basically, once one has studied the Buddhadharma and listened to the Sutras, one should not run down filthy roads again. In one's thoughts and actions one should be pure. AND KNOWING THOSE WHO HAVE MATURED/ AND THOSE WHO HAVE NOT YET MATURED/ For those who have not planted good roots, they help them to plant them. For those who have already planted good roots, they help them to grow. For those whose good roots have already grown, they help them to mature. THROUGH SUCH CALCULATIONS/ THEY DISCRIMINATE AND UNDERSTAND/ He knows the dispositions of living beings, AND IN THE PATHWAY OF ONE VEHICLE/ THEY APPROPRIATELY SPEAK OF THREE/ He speaks of the Three Vehicles.

Shakyamuni Buddha spoke the Dharma for forty-nine years in over three hundred Dharma Assemblies.

Index

THE BUDDHIST TEXT TRANSLATION SOCIETY

Chairperson: The Venerable Master Hua, Abbot of Gold Mountain
Monastery, Professor of the Tripitaka
and the Dhyanas

PRIMARY TRANSLATION COMMITTEE:
Chairpersons: Bhikshuni Heng Yin, Lecturer in Buddhism
Bhikshuni Heng Ch'ih, Lecturer in Buddhism

Members: Bhikshu Wei Sung, Lecturer in Buddhism
Bhikshu Heng Kuan, Lecturer in Buddhism
Bhikshu Heng Sure, Lecturer in Buddhism
Bhikshuni Heng Hsien, Lecturer in Buddhism
Bhikshuni Heng Ch'ing, Lecturer in Buddhism
Shramanerika Kuo Ching
Upasaka Huang Kuo-jen, Kung-fu Master, B.A.
Upasaka I Kuo-jung, Ph.D., U.C. Berkeley

REVISION COMMITTEE:

Chairperson: Upasaka I Kuo-jung

Members: Bhikshu Heng Kuan
Bhikshu Heng Sure
Bhikshuni Heng Yin
Bhikshuni Heng Hsien
Professor Lewis Lancaster, U.C. Berkeley
Professor M. Tseng, San Francisco State University
Upasaka Hsieh Ping-ying, author, professor, editor
Upasika Phoung Kuo-wu
Upasaka Lee Kuo-ch'ien, B.A.
Upasaka Li Kuo-wi, M.A.
Upasika I Kuo-han, B.A.
Upasika Kuo-ts'an Epstein
Upasika Kuo-chin Vickers

EDITORIAL COMMITTEE:

Chairperson: Bhikshu Heng Kuan

Members: Bhikshu Heng Sure
Bhikshu Heng Shun
Bhikshuni Heng Yin
Bhikshuni Heng Ch'ih
Bhikshuni Heng hsien
Bhikshuni Heng Chü
Bhikshuni Heng Ch'ing
Professor Irving Lo, University of Indiana

III.

THE BUDDHIST TEXT TRANSLATION SOCIETY

The Buddhist Text Translation Society is dedicated to making the genuine principles of the Buddhadharma available to the Western reader in a form that can be put directly into practice. Since 1972, the Society has been publishing English translations of Sutras, instructional handbooks in meditation and moral conduct, biographies, poetry, and fiction. Each of the Society's translations is accompanied by a contemporary commentary spoken by the Venerable Master Hsüan Hua. The Venerable Master Hua is the founder of Gold Mountain Monastery and the Institute for the Translation of Buddhist Texts, both located in San Francisco, as well as Gold Wheel Temple in Los Angeles, and the new center of world Buddhism, the City of Ten Thousand Buddhas, near Ukiah, California. The accurate and faithful translation of the Buddhist Canon into English and other Western languages is one of the most important objectives of the Sino-American Buddhist Association, the parent organization of the Buddhist Text Translation Society.

IV.

EIGHT REGULATIONS FOR TRANSLATION SOCIETY TRANSLATORS:

The translation of the Buddhist Tripitaka is a work of such magnitude that it could never be entrusted to a single person working on his own. Above all, translations of Sutras must be certified as the authentic transmission of the Buddha's proper Dharma. Translations done under the auspices of the Buddhist Text Translation Society, a body of more than thirty Sangha members and scholars, bear such authority. The following eight regulations govern the conduct of Buddhist Text Translation Society Translators:

1. A translator must free himself from motives of personal gain and reputation.

2. A translator must cultivate an attitude free from arrogance and conceit.

3. A translator must refrain from advertising himself and denigrating others.

4. A translator must not establish himself as the standard of correctness and supress the work of others with his fault-finding.

5. A translator must take the Buddha-mind as his own mind.

6. A translator must use the wisdom of the selective Dharma-eye to determine true principles.

7. A translator must request the Virtuous Elders from the ten directions to certify his translations.

8. A translator must endeavor to propagate the teachings by printing Sutras, Shastras, and Vinaya texts when his translations have been certified.

Also from BTTS:

With One Heart Bowing to the City of Ten Thousand Buddhas, Vol. I, Paperbound, with photos, 173 pages.

Listen to Yourself, Think Everything Over, Instruction in meditation and recitation.

Pure Land and Ch'an Dharma Talks, paperbound 72 pages.

Records of the Life of the Ven. Master Hsüan Hua, Vol. I, paperbound, 96 pages.

Records of the Life of the Venerable Master Hsüan Hua, Vol. II, paperbound, 229 pages.

World Peace Gathering, paperbound, 128 pages.

Three Steps One Bow, paperbound 156 pages.

The Ten Dharma Realms are Not Beyond a Single Thought, paperbound 72 pages.

Celebrisi's Journey, paperbound, 178 pages.

A BRIGHT STAR IN A TROUBLED WORLD:
THE CITY OF TEN THOUSAND BUDDHAS

Located at Talmage, California, just south of Ukiah and about two hours north of San Francisco, is Wonderful Enlightenment Mountain. Situated at the base is the 237 acre area holding 60 buildings which is called the City of Ten Thousand Buddhas which is fast becoming a center for religious, educational, and social programs for world Buddhism.

At present, the complex houses Tathagata Monastery and the Great Compassion House for men, Great Joyous Giving House for women, the campus of Dharma Realm Buddhist University, and a large auditorium. Plans are underway to present many kinds of programs to benefit people in spirit, mind, and body--a home for the aged, a hospital emphasizing the utilization of both eastern and western healing techniques, an alternative mental health facility, and educational programs ranging from pre-school through Ph.D. Cottage industries, organic farming, and living in harmony with our environment will be stressed. The City is an ideal spot for conventions where people of all races and religions can exchange their ideas and unite their energies to

Buddha-recitation at the City of Ten Thousand Buddhas

A Dharma lecture in the Hall of Ten Thousand Buddhas

promote human welfare and world peace.

Religious cultivation will be foremost and the City will be instrumental in the transmission of the orthodox precepts of the Buddhas, thus developing Bhikshus and Bhikshunis to teach and maintain the Buddhadharma. Rigorous cultivation sessions are held regularly and the grounds of the monastery provide a pure and quiet setting to pursue the study of meditation. A number of facilities are available for those found qualified to retreat into contemplative seclusion. The spacious grounds have more than a hundred acres of pine groves, and a running stream.

At a time when the world is torn with strife, the City of Ten Thousand Buddhas appears as a guiding star for all of us to discover life's true meaning and pass it on to future generations.

The four-fold assembly of disciples: City of Ten Thousand Buddhas

VII.

DHARMA REALM BUDDHIST UNIVERSITY

A SPECIAL APPROACH

Focus on Values: examining the moral foundations of ancient spiritual traditions, relating those traditions to space-age living, and finding what it takes to live in harmony with our social and natural environments.

Focus on change: a key to understanding ourselves, our relationships, and the crises of the modern world. What we seek is to be open to new ways of seeing ourselves, to new modes of relating to friend and stranger, and to new methods and technological aids that supplement and open up for us the limitless store of human wisdom, past and present.

Total environment education where teacher and student are partners in the educational process and share responsibility for it. Learning takes place both in and out of the classroom in a community which is concerned with the complex problems of society.

Personally tailored programs in which education need not be constricted by traditional department boundries. The emphasis will be on meaningful learning, not just the accumulation of facts and test-taking skills.

Education for young and old where the different generations come together to share in the experience of learning and thereby enrich that experience. The University also especially encourages those with valuable life experience to apply for special experimental learning credits.

GUIDING IDEALS

These are the ideals which will guide education at Dharma Realm University:

> *To explain and share the Buddha's teaching;*
> *To develop straightforward minds and hearts;*
> *To benefit society;*
> *To encourage all beings to seek enlightenment.*

CAMPUS

The main campus of Dharma Realm University is located at the foot of Cow Mountain National Recreation Area in the beautiful Ukiah valley. It is surrounded by the woods, meadows, and farm-land of the City of Ten Thousand Buddhas.

The University will be housed in several large buildings set among trees and broad lawns. One classroom building has been new-ly refurbished for educational use.

The air is clean and fresh, and the climate is pleasant and temperate (av. min. temp. 43.2 deg; av. max. temp. 76 deg.) Rare-ly falling below freezing in the winter and usually dry in the sum-mer, the area is very fertile with much grape and fruit tree cul-tivation. Close by are the Russian River, Lake Mendocino and Clear Lake, several hot springs, redwood and other national forest lands, and the scenic Pacific Coast.

PROGRAMS-Undergraduate and graduate, full-time and part-time

The University intends to provide quality education in a num-ber of fields, with   emphasis (wherever possible) on matching classroom theory with practical experience. The curriculum is divided into three main areas:

The Letters and Science Program: In addition to a regular curriculum of Humanities, Social, and Natural Sciences, special emphasis will be laid on East-West studies, with strong offerings in Asian languages, literature, philosophy, and religion. We ex-pect pioneering interdisciplinary approaches in many of these areas, combining the best of Asian and Western approaches to education. Education for personal growth and the development of special compe-tencies will be the twin aims of the program.

The Buddhist Studies Program will emphasize a combination of traditional and modern methods including actual practice of the Buddhadharma as well as scholarly investigation. Offerings will range from introductory fundamentals to advanced meditation and will include advanced seminars in both English and canonical lan-guages.

The Arts Program: Practical Arts will concentrate on putting knowledge to work right away in workshops for building a living community ecology, energy, gardening and nutrition, community planning, management, etc. Creative Arts offerings will include the meeting of East and West in a whole panorama of studio arts. There will be special courses in Chinese calligraphy, in the creation of Buddha images, and in music. Individual Arts workshops will include t'ai-chi ch'üan, yoga, meditational tech-niques, wilderness survival, and much more.

THE INTERNATIONAL TRANSLATION CENTER

The Translation Center will sponsor courses, workshops, and special programs concerned with translation techniques for a wide range of languages and will coordinate a unique degree program in translation.

THE WORLD RELIGIONS CENTER

The world Religions Center will sponsor workshops, conferences, and other special programs to aid in mutual understanding and good will among those of different faiths.

SPECIAL INTERNATIONAL STUDENT PROGRAM

In the future, there will be special emphasis on welcoming students from Asian countries to complement the University's strong offerings in East-West studies. Areas of special interest to Asian students will be added to the curriculum as well as a strong English as a Second Language (ESL) Program.

DONATIONS

Dharma Realm University welcomes your help with donations. In addition to financial assistance, the University needs home and office furniture, books and scholarly journals, supplies and equipment, and the services of volunteers. *All donations are tax deductable.*

VERSE ON RETURNING THE LIGHT

*Truly recognize your own faults
And don't discuss the faults of others.
Other's faults are just your own faults,
Being one with everyone
is called great compassion.*

— Ven. Master Hsuan Hua

PUBLICATIONS OF THE BUDDHIST TEXT TRANSLATION SOCIETY

BUDDHIST SUTRAS:

The Dharma Flower (Lotus) Sutra, with commentary. *"Those of slight widsom who delight in lesser dharmas do not believe that they can become Buddhas. That is why we (the Buddhas) use expedient methods, discriminating and teaching the various stages. Although three vehicles are taught, it is only for the sake of instructing Bodhisattvas".* The Lotus Flower of the Wondrous Dharma Sutra is the king of all Buddhist Sutras because it is the final teaching of the Buddha in which he proclaimed the ultimate and only vehicle- the Buddha-vehicle. Vol. 1, Introduction, 85 pgs. $3.95, Vol. II, 324 pgs. $7.95, Vol. III, $7.95 *Further volumes forthcoming.*

The Flower Garland (Avatamsaka) Sutra:

Preface by T'ang Dynasty National Master Ch'ing Liang. *"Going and returning without any trace; Movement and stillness have one source. Embracing the multitude of wonders yet more remains; Transcending words and thought by far. This can only be the Dharmarealm!"* The succint verse commentary to the Avatamsaka Sutra by the Venerable T'ang Dynasty Master present the Sutra's principles in concise and elegant form, explained for modern readers in the appended commentary by the Ven. Master Hua. $9.00 Tentative Price.

The Ten Dwellings, Chapter Fifteen with commentary. *"All dharmas are apart from words and speech. Their nature is empty, still, extinct and uncreated. Desiring to understand this principle of reality, the Bodhisattva resolves to become enlightened."* The major stages passed through by Bodhisattvas after an initial perfection of the Ten Faiths are: the Ten Dwellings, the Ten Practices, the Ten Transferences, the Ten Grounds, Equal Enlightenment and Wonderful Enlightenment. During the course of the Ten Dwellings the Bodhisattva truly brings forth the great thought for Bodhi, is reborn in the household of the Thus Come One, and receives Annointment of the Crown. $6.95

The Vajra Sutra, with commentary. *"All conditioned dharmas are like dreams, illusions, bubbles, shadows, like dew drops and a lightning flash; contemplate them thus."* Prajna or transcendental wisdom, the subject of this Sutra, is of central importance in the Buddha's teaching. The Buddha spent 20 years speaking the Prajna Sutras and declared that they would be disseminated to every land. 192 pgs. $8.00

The Amitabha Sutra, with commentary. *"Shariputra, if there is a good man or a good woman who hears spoken 'Amitabha' and holds his name, whether for one day, two days, three, four, five days, six days, as long as seven days. with one heart unconfused, when this person approaches the end of life, before him will appear Amitabha and all the assembly of holy ones. When the end comes, his heart will be without inversion; in Amitabha's Land of Ultimate Bliss he will attain rebirth."* Shakyamuni Buddha spoke the Amitabha Sutra to let all living beings know of the power of Amitabha Buddha's great vows to lead all who recite his name with faith to rebirth in his Buddhaland the Land of Ultimate Bliss, where they may cultivate and quickly realize Buddhahood. 204 pgs., $8.00

The Dharani Sutra, with commentary. *"World Honored One, I have a Great Compassion Dharani-mantra which I now wish to speak so that all living beings might obtain peace and delight, be rid of every sickness, and attain long life; so that they might obtain prosperity, wipe away the evil karma of heavy offenses, seperate themselves from obstacles and hardships, grow in all the pure dharmas and in every kind of merit and virtue."* In the Dharani Sutra, the Bodhisattva Avalokiteshvara (Gwan Yin) shows how by the practice of compassion and the recitation of the Great Compassion Mantra we can rescue living beings in distress by means of wholesome magic and healing. Illustrated with woodcuts from the Secret School. 352 pgs., $12.00

The Sutra in Forty-two Sections, with commentary. *"When the Shramana who has left the home-life puts an end to his desires and drives away his longings, he knows the source of his own mind and penetrates to the profound principles of Buddhahood. He awakens to the Unconditioned, clinging to nothing within and seeking nothing without."* The Sutra in which the Buddha gives the essentials of the Path. 114 pgs. $4.00